RUNNING, THINKING, WRITING

RUNNING, THINKING, WRITING

Embodied Cognition in Composition

Jackie Hoermann-Elliott

Parlor Press
Anderson, South Carolina
www.parlorpress.com

Parlor Press LLC, Anderson, South Carolina, USA
© 2021 by Parlor Press.
All rights reserved.
Printed in the United States of America on acid-free paper.

S A N: 2 5 4 - 8 8 7 9

Library of Congress Cataloging-in-Publication Data

Names: Hoermann-Elliott, Jackie, 1989- author.
Title: Running, thinking, writing : embodied cognition in composition /
    Jackie Hoermann-Elliott.
Description: Anderson, South Carolina : Parlor Press, [2021] | Includes
    bibliographical references and index. | Summary: "Provides a theoretical
    framework and descriptive profiles of professional and student writers
    that explain why so many writers like to run (or walk or move) and how
    physical activity improves thinking and writing"-- Provided by publisher.
Identifiers: LCCN 2021026527 (print) | LCCN 2021026528 (ebook) |
    ISBN 9781643172514 (paperback) | ISBN 9781643172521 (pdf) | ISBN
    9781643172538 (epub)
Subjects: LCSH: Running--Psychological aspects. | Mind and body. | Eng-
    lish language--Composition and exercises. | Philosophy of mind. Clas-
    sification: LCC GV1061.8.P75 H64 2021 (print) | LCC GV1061.8.P75
    (ebook) | DDC 796.4201/9--dc23
LC record available at https://lccn.loc.gov/2021026527
LC ebook record available at https://lccn.loc.gov/2021026528

2 3 4 5

978-1-64317-251-4 (paperback)
978-1-64317-252-1 (PDF)
978-1-64317-253-8 (EPUB)

Cover design by David Blakesley.
Cover photo by Cameron Venti on Unsplash.

Parlor Press, LLC is an independent publisher of scholarly and trade titles in
print and multimedia formats. This book is available in paper and ebook formats from Parlor Press on the World Wide Web at http://www.parlorpress.
com or through online and brick-and-mortar bookstores. For submission information or to find out about Parlor Press publications, write to Parlor Press,
3015 Brackenberry Drive, Anderson, South Carolina, 29621, or email edi-
tor@parlorpress.com.

Contents

For Buck, Elisabeth, Barrett, and Beau.
Thank you for keeping me on my toes.

Acknowledgments

When I first began this project, I remember Dr. Carrie Leverenz, my dissertation director, telling me, "Choose a research topic that you find really, really fascinating because you're going to be stuck with it for a while." Six years later, I am still enamored with embodied cognition's role in the writing process. I recognize that Carrie could have told me, an eager-to-please doctoral candidate at the time, to choose a research topic that would make me more appealing on the academic job market, but instead she nurtured my interest in embodiment. She led me toward my identity as a runner-writer-researcher, not away from it. I feel immense gratitude toward her for this gift of support she gave me (but will probably never take credit for).

Sitting second on my support bench is my partner, Buck. When the COVID-19 pandemic swept across our county and closed down our childcare facility, he did everything he could to give me time to write. Thank you to my children—Elisabeth, Barrett, and Beau—for understanding why mama had to escape to the porch to write in the afternoons.

While preparing this manuscript for publication, I suddenly lost my friend and colleague, Dr. Katie McWain. As I revised parts of this manuscript, I often thought of her encouraging voice or her sidesplitting laughter in response to something I had written. Thank you, Katie, for the million little glimmers of joy and friendship you continue to shine into my life. I wish you knew the influence you continue to have every day on my teaching, writing, and researching.

Special thanks are in order to my home department—the English, Speech, and Foreign Languages Department at Texas Woman's University—for supporting my book project in so many ways, including providing publication support funds to assist with the development of this manuscript and for assigning PhD candidate Meredith Pasahow to be my research assistant for this project. Meredith's editorial feedback made me smile from start to finish. Thank you, too, to my department chair

Dr. Genevieve West, for her never-ending empathy and mentorship. Genevieve, like Katie and Carrie, will forever be one of my sheroes.

Finally, I am grateful to Dr. David Blakesley for how approachable and friendly he was to work with as a publisher throughout this process as well as one of my outside reviewers, Stacy Cacciatore, who provided additional ideas for the expansion of this manuscript. My project has greatly benefited from the good-natured support and encouragement of the people of Parlor Press.

Running, Thinking, Writing

Introduction

In the second half of the twentieth century—just after the advent of jogging caught on in North America—a plenitude of studies followed confirming the impressive health benefits of regular running activity. From alleviating mental health burdens related to stress and depression to drastically improving blood pressure and cholesterol levels, moderate running has been shown to help the mind and the body flourish. Walking, another well-studied form of exercise involving a lower risk of injury, has also been shown to safeguard against a smattering of health conditions in addition to protecting against cognitive decline. These findings lead most scientists and scholars to believe that much of the cardiovascular exercises deemed good for the body are equally good for the health of the mind.

Yet with our attention turned to the physical and psychological effects of running and walking for so long, it seems as though we have jettisoned interest in the creative health benefits of these forms of exercise. For many writers, this interest is not one that is unknown or unfamiliar. In fact, writers as far back as antiquity reportedly used wrestling and other forms of physical exercise to hone their writing acumen (Hawhee 39). However, a recent surge of interest in the neurophysiological activity of the brain has uncovered that multiple brain structures assisting the mind in the act of writing may also be responsible for or enhanced by regular aerobic exercise (Hallett and Grafman, Erickson et al.). With these discoveries by neuroscientists and other discoveries made by cognitive scientists regarding the role of embodied cognition in the creative process, we stand to learn a great deal about how our brains thrive on exercise and how our writing processes might benefit as a welcome result of all our time spent in motion (McClelland, Osgood-Campbell).

For me, writing and running have never kept a respectable distance from each other. These two activities existed symbiotically, never moving along parallel lines in my life but instead intersecting and looping through each other repeatedly. I identify as a runner-writer, someone who uses their running time to benefit their writing time. While running, I craft ideas for my writing in tiny scraps and fragments, jotting these traces of insight down in scribbly, semi-cursive shorthand on a notepad at my desk so that when I am ready to return to my writing later—usually after a hot shower and a cold breakfast of overnight oats—they come to life once again. I have engaged in this habit since I began graduate school in 2011, when I remember several professors using running metaphors to explain long-term writing success habits to me. The oft-spoken "It's a marathon, not a sprint." adage was frequently plated and served, but for me running presented more than a metaphor for my writing. Something indescribable happened in my brain when I ran that improved my writing—even if I could not yet articulate what I experienced.

When *Atlantic* writer Nick Ripatrazone asked, "Why do writers so often love to run?" in 2015, I identified immediately. In the deck to a culture editorial he wrote titled "Why Writers Run," someone—most likely an editor or a copyeditor—tried to summarize Ripatrazone's findings as follows: "Racking up mile after mile is difficult, mind-expanding, and hypnotic—just like putting words down on a page."[1] In his article, Ripatrazone spills plenty of digital ink pondering why famous writers, such as Joyce Carol Oates, Jonathan Swift, and Louisa May Alcott, were cited as prodigal with pen in hand in part because they laced up their shoes for the sake of their writing practice.

Prior to the publication of Ripatrazone's think piece, the occasional rumbling would be raised about the relationship between running and writing activity, but the treatment of the topic would be superficial or fleeting at best. The possibility of running activity supporting one's writing activity had not been developed or challenged to the fullest extent possible. This book seeks to deepen our understanding of the relationship between writing and running, two similarly complex activities that necessitate intense focus, at times, and a strong sense of motivation. For the betterment of writers who identify as runners and walkers, or any person using their physical body to engage in other means of motion, this book uncovers the varied understandings of the relationship between writing activity and physical activity. For what purpose? We all share one common goal: building up our writing mileage. We all seek to move forward with our work as writers. When stagnancy strikes or when a writing task feels daunting, we physically move to keep our writing minds moving forward, too.

As a writing researcher, I have always been interested in the body at work. Perhaps this is because I am a fidgeter—not the leg quaking kind that hardly notices when their shaking is bothering others, but a head-scratching, slow toe-tapping, brow-furrowing writer who has to move to think. I have always noticed these movements in myself and others and wondered what these physical manifestations of my mind might mean for my work and the work of others. Countless times I have been in writing retreats or workshops working alongside other writers, and I have watched how they position their bodies as they work. The body, when it is at work writing, moves into the piece. Shoulders hunch a little too far forward, eyes lock in focus, energy travels outward to the extremities, released in the form of tapping, shaking, and shifting. Sometimes, when the words won't come anymore, I see writers grip something: a pen, a piece of chocolate, an appendage, or sometimes even a friend. If you have ever been in a room full of writers writing or if you have ever had a friend invite you to a writing date at a coffee shop, then you know what I mean when I say that your dearest friend suddenly becomes the greatest deterrent to your success, telling you everything you did not need to know about their most recent success in kombucha-making or showing you cat pictures. These are signs the writing is not going well.

Another sign I often see is writers getting out of their seats and pacing or taking a bathroom break. The difference between your struggling-to-write-but-not-to-talk friend and the fellow writer who literally steps away from the laptop is an important one, though, and one I remain interested in. When we move during a writing session or when we interrupt our writing process with small physical movements, we are reminded that our writing minds exist as part of larger writing bodies. We feel much-needed release from the grips of our writing processes, at times, and at other times we move away from our writing station because we desperately need to reconnect with our intentions for a writing session, the ones we carried in the door but may have scuttled out of the room for some reason.

Spend enough time with a group of dedicated professional writers and you will likely find that a few are avid runners. These runner-writers are quick to self-identify and even quicker to indulge you in a conversation about either of their two loves, the running or the writing, because both pastimes define how they seem themselves. Some are quick to offer a comparison of running and writing, but that is where the conversation starts to trail off. An analogy made. A look of insight recognized. The topic of conversation meanders elsewhere.

I do not mean to suggest that all or even the best writers are runners, but all writers are embodied writers and thinkers. Running, I have found, is a form of physical activity many writers find conducive to their creative processes, and I will explore in depth how running can support a writer's writing. Other forms of moving, however, can induce creativity in equally meaningful ways. My aim in this book is to share what my research revealed, which is that, on the one hand, some professional writers who exercise become adept at using embodied cognition strategies to enhance productivity and creativity. On the other hand, I also found that novice and student writers mentally resist connecting movement to writing, considering the latter a purely sedentary practice. The title of this book, *Running, Thinking, Writing: Embodied Cognition in Composition*, gives nod to what were once thought to be radical claims about writing made by Ann E. Berthoff. In her book, *Forming, Thinking, Writing*, Berthoff brings to our attention her theory on the active mind as forming ideas and seeing relationships for the purposes of writing all the time, saying, "Many of the psychologically troubling aspects of composing can be dealt with by developing work habits, which can include giving in to harmless compulsions if they make you feel more comfortable" (262). A compulsion as harmless as recreational running, for example, might assist those writers who desperately struggle with writer's block, procrastination, or lack of inspiration.

Each chapter begins with a nested narrative in which I reflect on past connections I have made between my body and my writing for the purposes of bringing the reader into an up-close-and-personal moment when I have profoundly felt the effects of embodied cognition. These personal anecdotes are not stacked up in chronological order, but rather, selectively feathered into the start of the chapter where they feel most needed. In a way, these anecdotes are as pedagogical as they are personal. As a feminist pedagogue, I have made the conscious decision to include these nested narratives as a way of bringing the reader closer to my life and work, exposing moments of personal triumph and failure for the sake of authentically connecting theory to lived experience.

In Chapter One, "Warming Up: An Introduction to Embodied Writing in Writing Studies," I take readers from cognitivist roots in writing research to contemporary ideas of embodied cognition in composing (embodied or contemplative writing). Through my exploration of other writing scholars' findings, I position my readers to see the historical formation of relevant foundational claims about embodied cognition's role in the writing process.

In Chapter Two, "The First Lap: A Trek through Embodied Cognition," I take the metaphor in the chapter title somewhat literally, acting as a guide wading through philosophies outside of writing studies that informed much of my project's methodology and design. I introduce a new theoretical framework for embodied writing, one that features three key concepts—generative knowing, restorative knowing, and knowledge structuring—define what writers experience when they think about their writing in connection to their movement. These concepts, I argue, hold great potential for increased creativity and productivity in the work of all writers.

Chapter Three, "In the Zone: Research on Walking and Running," provides a foundational understanding of the mechanics of walking as a first progression toward running. The differences between the two activities are elaborated in separate sections that unpack and compare the neurological and psychological benefit of walking and running for most writers' creativity. I also take time to unearth new data on the whiteness of running culture as well as the diversity issues that impact who can run safely in public outdoor spaces. The title of this chapter refers to the state of being "in the zone" or deeply entranced in a physical endeavor in much the same way one can become engrossed in writing of any form and at any level. I aim to explain what this zone is and how it may benefit the embodied writer.

By Chapter Four, "The Mind Flies: An Embodied Cognition Framework for Analysis," I have formally introduced a framework through which we can understand my three new conceptual terms for understanding the relationship between physical activity and writing activity, and I apply those terms in an analysis of work by well-known authors commenting on this relationship.

Having equipped the reader to understand and apply the terms I have fashioned for the purposes of understanding embodied writing, I leap into Chapter Five, "Going Pro: Portraits of Successful Embodied Writers." In this chapter, I paint four colorful portraits of professional writers who also happen to be dedicated runners and for whom the relationship between physical activity and writing activity must be approached intentionally. These runner-writers, include Brentney Hamilton, a *Dallas Morning News* journalist who runs marathons and ultramarathons; Dr.

Jordan Smith, an assistant professor of technical communication who runs, walks, and lifts weights; Christie Wright Wild, a children's book author and novelist who teaches adult writers to connect their running experiences to their professional work as writers at her annual summer retreat; and Dr. Thomas Gardner, a professor of literature and lyrical essayist, who of all my runner-writer participants has the most marathons under his belt. These portraits bring into fuller view the scholarship outlined in previous chapters while extracting colorful clips for further analysis of what embodied cognition holds for all writers when we apply the new theoretical concepts offered in the previous chapter. To be very clear, I define a professional writer as any individual who 1) regularly publishes writing online or in print text documents for general consumption, or 2) someone for whom writing is a significant aspect of their career experience. Traditional print authors were counted as professional writers for having published one or more articles, chapters, features, poems, or book-length texts, including academic authors who are required to publish for tenure and promotion.

Chapter Six, "Learning Hurdles: Novice Writers Practicing Embodied Writing," calls attention to a different group of writers: college students. In focusing on students who have grown accustomed to writing in disembodied contexts—namely, seated at desks or in classrooms—I share the experiences of a few young women, each of whom was enrolled in writing courses I taught at Texas Christian University or Texas Woman's University. I call attention to the most powerful moments when these novice writers struggle to engage the body in the writing process, to think about writing while moving, walking, and even running, and when they triumph in the deeply engaged, powerful moments of embodied cognition. Additionally, I discuss how the concepts in my theoretical framework function differently for those who are coming to learn the craft of writing. My main claim in this chapter is that the ideation, creation, and production of writing is possible for novice writers through careful practice and encouragement.

Finally, in Chapter Seven, "Finding the Finish: Recommendations for Writing with the Body," I review my findings while supporting claims about the benefits of an embodied writing process for writers of all ability levels. For teachers of writing, I make pedagogical recommendations for incorporating physical movement into the classroom and for developing lesson plans that engage and support students with a range of bodily abilities—to be inclusive of all writers who can and cannot run. Ultimately, I conclude this chapter by returning to my central argument: All writers can be more creative and productive when they tap into physical practices that support embodied cognition in connection to the writing process.

So why do writers so often love to run? Or walk? Or engage in any other form of physical activity? This book begins to uncover a kaleidoscopic assortment of possibilities for all writers, especially those who have felt compelled to think about their writing while running or engaged in another form of sensorimotor movement. When writers tap down deep into the bone-level, latent potential of embodied cognition, the creative and productive potential for their work is limitless.

1 Warming Up: An Introduction to Embodied Writing in Writing Studies

Turning the corner of 9th Street, I feel the cool touch of fall on my forehead and the tops of my exposed shoulders. "I'll need a jacket soon." I think to myself. "How early is early when the Iowans say, 'Fall comes early in Iowa'?" My arms pull forward and backward as if they were meant to stay in this motion for a millennia or more, breathing in the earthy scent of leaves crisping with brown at the edges of fiery red and orange points, falling around the perfectly landscaped edges of a street of 1930s-era homes. I turn to admire one of my favorite homes in Ames—a boxy blue two-story built in the Roosevelt neighborhood. The flat stacked stones are a light grey that appears almost white in the September sunshine. This particular gated stone bed reminds me of those I used to run alongside in Kansas City's Brookside neighborhood, back when I was at my most sedentary, sitting for days on end as I wrote my senior honors thesis on recalcitrant antebellum nuns.

Now, here in Iowa, the impulse to run feels different, like I'm searching for a part of myself I don't know yet. This new part of me feels older but more energetic. I feel confined by the commitment I made to living in Ames and working on my master's degree at Iowa State University, but I can't help but feel an expansiveness, too, a kind of premature sense of satisfaction with the prospect of writing my master's thesis in a year—even though I haven't jotted down a single note yet.

That's why I'm running. I'd already mentally wallpapered most of the faux stucco finish walls in my one-bedroom apartment with far too many ideas this morning. I needed to get out. I needed a reason to get outside of my designated dwelling space and out of my head. And yet, as I started jogging out of the southeast quadrant of this town to head to the park, the ideas kept coming, one-by-one, grander and more involved than the one before, until I surrendered to one. And when I did, it felt effortlessly indulgent and satisfying. I entertained thesis ideas like these:

> Maybe my thesis should be about visual rhetorical analysis instruction in the first-year composition classroom? I think that's going to be my favorite genre to teach.
>
> But I also think I want to direct a writing program one day. Or do I? I just don't know that I want to write about administration yet. How can I without any recent experience?
>
> Then again, email communication is so fascinating. Why don't we teach email in composition courses?
>
> Does anyone find email as interesting as I do? Probably not. I should probably analyze a strong female rhetor. I could return to Catholic women rhetors.
>
> If I write about Catholic rhetorics, will my parents read my thesis?
>
> Will anyone ever read my thesis?

My mind feels like it's tripping over a rug so folded that it'll never be flat unless I stop and redirect my attention elsewhere.

Bubbling over with physical exuberance, I breathe in through my nose to see if I can feel the chilling burn of winter's air. Not yet. A cool, sunny fall run must be one of the most life-affirming feelings a person can take comfort in, I think. Several months from now, I'll hold onto this thought as I jog through treacherously icy footpaths, inadequately dressed to meet these unfamiliar and bitterly cold elements, and I won't be able to invent ideas for my writing at all, not when a light freezing rain stings my quads enough to make me wonder if I'll see signs of frostbite on my legs when I arrive at home. (I will.) No writing happens on runs with terrible weather. My mind can't wander when my body is in pain.

When I turn right to head toward Brookside Park, I tell myself that I should stop and write down these ideas. I fear losing them. I also fear returning to them and feeling like the words I've sent in little SMS messages to myself will feel devoid of meaning, lacking in feeling or force when I look at them again from the comfort of my desk. Will these words help me later? Will I feel discouraged? How will I return to this feeling of excitement about writing in a genre that most quail at? I don't know. What I do know is that I'll call my father later and tell him that I matched his longest distance: seven miles complete at slightly less than a ten-minute-per-mile pace. What I've also come to know is this: My writing found a way into my running, and I've been chasing the writing ever since.

INTRODUCTION

In my research in the field of writing studies, relatively few researchers have inquired into the relationship between moving bodies and writing bodies. Published scholarship on this relationship tends to be difficult to find, highly variable in focus, and sometimes lacking in the scholarly terminology needed to define the nuanced ways writers embody their writing and describe their writing in embodied terms. I have often wondered if this is the case because writing researchers have hesitated to venture into other disciplines, such as kinesiology or sports psychology, or if researchers in these other disciplines could not care less about how movement plays a role in the writing process. Nevertheless, we are left with important questions we must ask ourselves before embarking on a long journey through available research from seemingly disparate disciplines: What is the relationship between literate practices, specifically writing activity, and non-literate practices, specifically physical activity? How does the regular practice of disciplined physical activity affect writing activity and performance?

To answer these questions, a review of relevant literature is needed. What I can offer the reader in this chapter is a bouquet of scholarly findings all related to embodied writing, picked from the field of writing studies, first and foremost, but often borrowing information or inspiration from various disciplines and subdisciplines, including embodied cognition and kinesiology. Our forays into these other fields support a holistic understanding of this relationship in all its mental-physical-intellectual complexity. Toward that end, I will sketch out relevant theories and empirical data that demonstrate the potential for cross-talk in the fields of writing studies, psychology, kinesiology, and more so that we might explore our shared theoretical ground, from which many of the new theoretical concepts I offer will be derived.

EMBODIED COGNITION IN WRITING STUDIES

The field of writing studies is at an interesting juncture in its history as more scholars gravitate toward a new pedagogical subfield, known as embodied writing, that often invites movement and embodied cognition into the writing classroom. A somewhat recent definition of embodied cognition from compositionists came in 2016 when Charles Bazerman and Howard Tinberg claimed that embodied cognition was a threshold concept for writers:

> If cognition assumes complex mental processes at work, then embodied cognition draws in addition upon the physical and affective aspects of the composing process. While there is still much to learn about how the brain and mind work when engaged in the complex task of writing, it was evident to theorists as early as James Moffett (1968) and Ann Berthoff (1978; 1981) that writing comes from full engagement of the entire writer, which is developed across many years of a developing self. (74)

Bazerman and Tinberg's definition is not overtly physical, nor does it define the sensory or motor movements of particular types of embodied writing to any great lengths, but it is the most recent and comprehensive definition of embodied cognition presented by writing scholars to date. What is also interesting about this definition is the mention of affective aspects involved in embodied cognition, meaning that this definition accounts for an emotional quotient not often considered when coming to learn embodied cognition, but one that is no less relevant or promising in our quest to better understand the body's role in writing.

Before Bazerman and Tinberg staked any sort of claim about writing and embodiment as interconnected, though, ancient teachers of writing and rhetoric—writing's disciplinary sibling—were practicing the "full engagement of the entire writer." As far back as antiquity, the body was considered integral to thinking and writing well. Plato is thought to have once said, "In order for man to succeed in life, God provided him with two means, education and physical activity. Not separately, one for the soul and the other for the body, but for the two together. With these two means, man can attain perfection."[2] Health of body and mind are inextricably bound up in Plato's conception of a successful person. Like the marbling of connective tissue that yokes muscle to bone, deciphering precisely where the boundaries of body and mind begin or end can prove difficult since one depends on the other to function effectively. Isocrates makes a similar comparison in one of his well-known works, *Antidosis*, circa 354 BCE (201). Of body and mind, Isocrates writes:

> These are twin arts—parallel and complementary—by which their masters prepare the mind to become more intelligent and

the body to become more serviceable, not separating sharply the
two kinds of education, but using similar methods of instruction, exercise, and other forms of discipline. For when they take
their pupils in hand, the physical trainers instruct their followers in the postures which have been devised for bodily contests,
while the teachers of philosophy impart all the forms of discourse in which the mind expresses itself.

Although he states earlier in the piece that the mind is superior to the
body, Isocrates draws the two activities metaphorically nearer to one another in the ancient classroom, which would have looked nothing like
the desk-rowed classrooms of contemporary learning environments. Students were not expected to sit still in a chair through a lesson, but rather, to move their bodies in the palestras that supported their embodied
learning. Greco-style palestras were elaborately designed gymnasiums
where physical and intellectual training took place, and scholar Debra
Hawhee was one of the first twenty-first century American scholars to
re-orient audiences to the sites and the purpose of these embodied past
practices of rhetoric and writing instruction.[3]

Returning to Bazerman and Tinberg's writing-specific conceptual-
ization of embodied cognition, these authors reference the more contemporary theories of Ann Berthoff, a writing studies scholar who coins the
term muscular imagination in 1984, which enriched the Montessorian
concept of muscle memory with "analogy to actual movement" (*Reclaiming the Imagination* 25). Berthoff offers this term in a very literal sense,
not a metaphorical sense, to convey a physical rhythm of writing "closely
allied with 'bodily' processes" (25). To Berthoff, all "rhythmic experiences" in writing employ muscular imagination through "analog[ies] to
actual movement, since sounds may rise and fall, and in a remote way
one rises and falls with them" (25). Berthoff claims that even prose writing has a rhythm writers seek to establish and that once writers move forward through their writing processes, they sense and develop rhythms of
wordplay and syntax their writing needs, comparing the writer's achieve-
ment of rhythm and flow to that of "sauntering" smoothly through a
crowd of people (25). The muscular imagination that moves an athlete
through a physical activity also moves a writer through writing activity.
Conceptually, the idea of embodied cognition incubates as a seedling in
Berthoff's thoughts on muscular imagination, especially in her unforget-
table comparison of writing to skiing. In 1990, Berthoff wrote another
book, *The Sense of Learning*, in which she briefly asserts that "motor

behavior" may aid writers. She writes about a time when she failed to understand the directions of her ski instructor:

> Let me speak from my experience as a profoundly unathletic person . . . [My ski instructor's instruction was to do thus and do so with my knees, to hold my arms this way and not that way, etc.] All that happened was that I continually pitched forward and fell in the snow. But suddenly across the meadows, I saw a figure going like the wind—a young man in shorts and a tee shirt, obviously a serious skier! And as I watched I suddenly saw the whole shape of the act of skiing; I saw the Gestalt; I got the rhythm, the allatonceness of the action. I did what I saw and I shot across the snow! What I needed was not a *model* which could show me how the various gestures and stances and operations fitted together, but an image of how cross-country skiing *looks*, and kinesthetically, how it *feels*. The image of the skier gave me the whole process; it represented the allatonceness of cross-country skiing. (89)

By way of this story about physical activity, Berthoff is attempting to convey a concept of writing called allatonceness. Of all the possible analogies she could have used to depict allatonceness, I find it fascinating that she chose an analogy focusing on the physical feeling of skiing. With this analogy, she elegantly describes what it feels like to be in a state of flow in which all conditions of an activity are working simultaneously to optimize the outcome of either a writing or physical experience, and she demonstrates how a writer discovers physical rhythm that can be translated into the writer's writing activity. Although she doesn't arrange for an equally elaborate anecdote to define how skiers can use their experiences with writing to improve their skiing activity, she is laying important groundwork for the field to gather and discuss the implications of embodied cognition using an embodied experience to relay her experiences as a writer. In her account, she never formally names the phenomenon she describes, but we, as writers and writing scholars, can appreciate the way in which her brief mention of muscular imagination in *Reclaiming the Imagination* has become more sophisticated six years later in this mention of the concept in *The Sense of Learning*.

Around the same time Berthoff theorized about muscular imagination and allatonceness, Walter J. Ong also grounded arguments about embodiment in the context of his research on orality's role in writing.

In *Orality and Literacy: The Technologizing of the Word*, Ong arrives at the idea of embodiment, alluding to how embodiment is particularly central to good speaking abilities (67). As he argues, refined speaking abilities continue to refine or improve a rhetor's writing abilities. Therefore, the uniquely embodied nature of speaking ought to be considered more thoughtfully with writing activities, too. At one point, he notes that when writing occurs, "the whole body labors" (Ong 95). This claim presents ample opportunity to think about how various body parts may seem to be at rest but are in fact at work while the body is writing. That is, one can imagine that Ong appreciated how the backs of even the most sedentary writers may have ached with poor posture or hung with fatigue over a desk after hours of sitting. The eyes must focus intently in front of them. The brow may furrow in deep thought, and the neck strain forward as intensity builds during a writing session. On the contrary, Ong could have been referring to the fact that some bodies rise and move from the desk as a way of generating ideas for writing creation and revision. The point is that the body is involved in the process of writing, even though its presence is rarely discussed or understood.

In their 1999 collection, *Rhetorical Bodies*, Jack Selzer and Sharon Crowley described the role of non-literate embodied actions in shaping the literate practices of writing. After much discussion and drafting with a cadre of contributors who shared an interest in embodied rhetorics and writing practices, they put forth a most compelling account:

> Contributors insist that material, nonliterate practices and realities—most notably, the body, flesh, blood, and bones, and how all the material trappings of the physical are fashioned by literate practices—should come under rhetorical scrutiny to demonstrate 'the material circumstances that sustain [literate practices].' (10)

Rhetorical Bodies presented the field with research and theory to support the existence of a relationship between physical practices and "literate practices," firmly suggesting that physical practices, such as delivering a speech or reading someone's body language, are shaped by literate practices—as seen in the chapter on working-class women contemplating their bodies through poetry. A few contributors discuss how existing in disabled bodies challenges traditional approaches to writing work or rhetorical creation, but none of the contributors explores the potential benefits of able-bodied physical activity for academic writers. What this contribution does not reveal is how concepts from embodied cognition or embodied writing pedagogy are being used to help students generate new knowledge as part of their writing processes or how students might come to understand the dynamic relationship between physical activity and writing activity. Thus, my research redirects scholarly attention away from the limitations of bodies, focusing instead on how sensorimotor ability at any level enables bodies to optimize during the writing process.[4]

Given writing studies researchers' proximity to undergraduate student populations, a surprisingly paltry number of studies have been conducted to explore the relationship between writing and movement for student-athletes. One of the most robust examples hails from Julie Cheville. In *Minding the Body: What Student Athletes Know about Learning*, Cheville interviews and observes members of the women's basketball team at the University of Iowa and one football player, arguing that teachers need to see student athletes as more than bodies that perform well at athletic endeavors. Instead, she argues that once we recognize the potential of embodied cognition, we will be able to "understand the body as vital to learning and thought [creation]" (Cheville 108, 138). Cheville calls on scholars to investigate the concept of embodied cognition as a "guiding principle" for learning in the first-year composition classroom (138–39). For Cheville, embodied cognition refers to the physical orientation of the body "in the contexts of [an] activity [that] determines what cognitive structures are available to learners" (8). A subordinate claim to her larger argument is that learning is a critical aspect of any athletic enterprise, and both a student or an athlete's success in learning to write in a new way and learning to practice a new movement technique in their sport require a high level of discipline. Cheville lauds discipline as a necessity for optimal performance, defining both the disciplined athlete and writer as similar, needing to "submi[t] him- or herself to the power of a particular way of knowing/behaving in order to participate in that power, to become more effective in applying it and thus to gain the satisfaction and rewards that it offers," including athletic or written prowess, competitive standing, or critical acclaim, to name just a few" (64). Thus, discipline becomes a desirable trait to nurture in both physical activity and writing activity, so much so that she opens the door for researchers, such as myself, to compare the two activities and wonder how writers can use physical movement to support and sustain lifelong writing.[5]

A resurgence of disciplinary interest in the ancient Western approach to teaching body and mind inspired Debra Hawhee's 2004 book, *Bodily Arts: Rhetoric and Athletics in Ancient Greece*, which offers a thorough historical treatment of writing performance reinforced through physical performance in the gymnasia of ancient Greece. Hawhee's research into ancient wrestling practices found that these practices were held alongside or in conjunction with rhetorical instruction practices (39). In keeping with the beliefs of Plato and Isocrates, mentioned earlier in this chapter, Hawhee uncovers the lost pedagogical art of supporting the combination of these physical and writing activities so that students might contemplate and enact the metaphors of physical moves mimicked or mirrored in their finessing of rhetorical moves and writing techniques learned in classrooms (147). Still somewhat novel to rhetoric and writing instructors who were groomed to teach in disembodied contexts, Hawhee's research reinvigorated interest in ancient mind-body writing practices, and yet, since then only a handful other scholars have expanded her research by investigating the relationship between physical activity and writing activity—neither in ancient nor contemporary contexts.

RECENT INTEREST IN EMBODIED WRITING

In 2004, Sondra Perl explored the cognitive aspects of writing that could not be accounted for by the then popular think-aloud protocols developed by Linda Flower and John R. Hayes ("Understanding Composing"). More specifically, Perl found that Flower and Hayes's findings on the cognitive process theory of writing needed more embodied research and contextualization in order to account for another sense of learning that was difficult to describe. This gap in the field of writing studies knowledge led Perl to define felt sense, an experience of bodily awareness that allows us to understand how felt senses "[encompass] everything you feel and know about a given subject at a given time. . . . It is felt in the body, yet has meanings. It is the mind and body before they split apart" (364).[6] Felt sense explains how a writer perceives a topic, word, or idea through bodily feeling, a visceral connection to the idea that takes on many different forms or sensations, such as how one holds one's posture while writing excitedly or anxiously or how a writer feels in their gut when approaching a daunting writing task. In this article, Perl delivers one of her most inspiring conclusions: "[felt senses] leave us with the potential for creating even more powerful ways of understanding composing" (369). Although her contribution of the concept of felt sense was pivotal in naming what scholars had only previously discussed conjecturally or uncomfortably, she called attention to the same ideas of embodied cognition before writing studies scholars were aware such a concept existed.

Throughout the next two decades, Perl would gain followers who enthusiastically approached her about the idea of felt sense but who also admitted they needed more help understanding the concept if they were going to teach students how to harness felt senses in the classroom (Perl *Felt Sense* xiii). After leading several workshops—and some championing by Peter Elbow and other expressivists—Perl published *Felt Sense,* a book with an audio companion of prompts for attending to one's felt sense before, during, and after the physical act of writing begins. In the first chapter, she describes more explicitly what qualifies as a felt sense experience:

> Maybe your body tingles. You love what is happening and wish there were some way to hold on to this experience. . . . When the words are emerging right, we often feel excited or at least pleased; we experience a kind of flow. Physically and mentally, we are aligned. (3)

In the beginning and throughout her book, Perl returns to the role of the body while writing. Having previously identified herself as a cognitivist, she marks her transition into new, unchartered sensorimotor territory to show how writing is an embodied act. Her mention of writing as a "kind of flow" experience is striking. If we are to think about how athletes say they need to "get in the zone" to perform at their best physically, how different, then, is this statement from a writer saying she or he needs to "get into the flow" of writing? These phrases are not exclusive to writers or athletes; in fact, I have heard athletes talk about their flow and writers talk about being in their writing zone. I, for one, have used both phrases to discuss my writing when it is going well. The actual phrases used—be it "flow," "get in the zone," or another phrase—matter little; conceptually, the idea remains the same. How might we hold onto the importance of the idea of "flow" from Perl's felt sense approach? With conscious attention being paid to this feeling, we might connect the flow-like feeling of felt sense to writing in the physical practices of yoga, running, and other physical endeavors.

Kristie Fleckenstein and Carolina Mancuso have claimed that there is an elusive "physicality to writing" that when experienced can support and improve the activity of writers as they work toward their goals ("Writing Yogis" 26). For example, walking meditations are one type of embodied action used to focus the mind and loosen the flow of creativity. Yet quite a few of the greatest writers have been depicted in sedentary positions, rarely pictured or discussed for their great love of running, walking, or engaging in other sorts of physical activities.[7]

Fortunately, scholars such as Robert Yagelski argue in favor of the immense benefits of physical movement for student and professional writers in his book, *Writing as a Way of Being: Writing Instruction, Non-duality, and the Crisis of Sustainability.* Yagelski locates the limitations of sedentarism in recent educational history. He paints all-too-familiar images of students sitting for most of the day at desks, heads down, eyes fixed just a few inches in front of them, floundering in the forced stillness of the contemporary classroom. He draws on the findings of others to fault standardized testing and neoliberal political initiatives, such as "Race to The Top," as complicit in fostering a "dualistic Cartesian sense of self" (Yagelski 12). That is, the federally mandated pressure to pass competency tests has shifted focus away from educating the whole person—in body, mind, and spirit equally—commanding instead that the intelligent being develops her mind first and foremost, in keeping with Cartesian philosophy: "I think, therefore I am." However, relying on assessment ushers in a "process of disembodiment that both reflects and reinforces the Cartesian self . . . [as being] separate from the physical environment" (Yagelski 18–19). Toward the end of his book, Yagelski argues that "language—and therefore writing—does not separate us from the physical but expresses our physicalness, our materiality, our oneness with the world" (95). Yagelski provides anecdotal and historically based evidence to demonstrate how discussions of the body cannot be extracted from the process of writing. The body can be ignored, certainly, but never fully removed from the writing environment.

Yagelski's work fits within a growing subfield of writing studies that includes scholars writing about embodied cognition that has most commonly been referred to as contemplative or embodied writing pedagogy and has become one of the focal points of scholarly interest in the *Journal for the Assembly for Expanded Perspectives on Learning* (JAEPL). Best defined by Christy Wenger, contemplative writing—which in earlier research projects Wenger referred to as embodied writing pedagogy—supports the "meaningful transfer of skills," such as writing, by "using the embodied insights from contemplative practices such as yoga, meditation, and the martial arts, among others, and fusing them with a traditional curriculum" (*Yoga Minds* 10–11). I favor the use of the phrase embodied writing pedagogy because although one could argue that all embodied writing activity is contemplative, the findings in this study turn our attention toward more deeply physical practices (away from strictly sensorimotor physical movements that require writers to sit still). Also, the phrase contemplative writing pedagogy includes research and pedagogical methods that utilize far more spiritual than physical practices. Although physical practices are certainly a part of the contemplative writing movement, I want to be clear that I am looking at embodied writing more generally and in a uniquely sensorimotor way that fits with popular definitions of flow and embodied cognition used in other fields.

To bring to a close this jaunt through ancient history to more recent work on embodied cognition in writing studies, we should look at the recent work of Jennifer Lin LeMesurier, who recently found common theoretical ground between embodied cognition and composition. In "Mobile Bodies: Triggering Bodily Uptake through Movement," she argues that "[w]e need to reconsider how the ways we speak about bodily practices in the composition classroom do or do not support the metacognitive frameworks we also model" (293). She applies two critical adjectives when explaining the relationship between writing activity and physical activity, *reflexive* and *bidirectional*, which factor into how writers deploy knowledge "through bodily memory" (297). After interviewing four embodied student writers, all dancers, LeMesurier describes the connection they see between writing activity and physical activity as a process of bodily uptake, which she defines as: "A process that relies on the ability to shift bodily intention in the moment of reperformance . . . less an instance of situational disguise and more a process of activating latent bodily expertise" (299). More specifically, she describes bodily uptake as more of a habit or habitual process established by a person's history of movement patterns that results in "strategic bodily iteration" that enables that person "to maneuver through the expectations of other bodies, texts, and affects in a given situation," such as writing (313). From the dancers she interviewed, the most prominent findings from LeMesurier's research include the insufficiency of metacognition research for "unpacking" what we "meta-embodiedly attend to" as we write. She encourages scholars to continue "tackl[ing] this conundrum through considering how we accumulate traces of situational knowledge that support rhetorical dexterity in part by the uptakes they condition and secure" (LeMesurier 314). LeMesurier's theorizing of bodily uptake helps us identify the relationship between writing and physical activity in a general sense, aligning with A. Abby Knoblauch's larger framework for understanding embodied cognition.

Knoblauch's Framework

If the last few decades have taught us anything about embodied cognition research's connection to writing studies, it is that there is a growing queue of writing studies researchers and theorists lining up to discuss this growing subfield of the discipline. Few have been able to offer, however, a comprehensive framework for delineating concepts within this subfield. A. Abby Knoblauch, however, has tendered a new framework for understanding the ways in which scholars, writers, and teachers talk about embodiment. Her framework outlines three distinct and overarching categories of embodiment within rhetoric and writing studies as a whole: embodied language, embodied knowledge, and embodied rhetoric.

First, with embodied language, she models how and what this category constitutes by using and then referring back to examples of embodied language in her own text. Knoblauch describes how the categories "bleed into each other" and how she "flesh[es] out" terminology (52). She cites commonly used verbs to inspire our thinking about how our everyday uses of language, even those that are less metaphorical, stem from an embodied understanding of our physical beings, such as "wrestle" and "embrace" (52). This language, she claims, "speaks to and from bodies, it can carry multiple meanings, acting as a catalyst for both identification and disidentification" (52). In later chapters, I will further elaborate on and analyze more examples of embodied language that support Knoblauch's claim for this category.

The second category in this framework is one we will spend the most time with because it brings into fuller view the grounded theory findings from my research. Embodied knowledge is more abstract and sometimes more difficult to parse than embodied language or embodied rhetoric, but Knoblauch confirms that overlap between all three is an inherent quality of our inquiry into embodiment. Embodied knowledge can be thought of as distinct from embodied language. To wit, Knoblauch defines embodied knowledge as "knowledge that is very clearly connected to the body," frequently beginning with the feeling of a "bodily response" or even a "gut reaction" that results in making meaning (54). We make meaning with and through the body, conferring with our sensations before transferring what we learn from our sensations into other contexts in which we need to make knowledge.

In this category, working from a platform for embodied knowledge production begets a generative force that benefits the writer (Knoblauch 56). This generative force enables the writer to invent, to write, or to revise because she or he is generating new knowledge from the platform of their body, relating out to their writing from a place of embodied understanding. What is generative is seen in the accumulation of ideas, words, and even additions or subtractions of text that bring the writer nearer to creating a textual body. Before I unearthed Knoblauch's definition of embodied knowledge as it pertains to generative force, my application of grounded theory principles while coding led me to arrive at a similar term—generative thinking—as well as a counterpart term—restorative thinking—both of which will be extrapolated in Chapter Four.

The third and final category in Knoblauch's framework, embodied rhetoric, is one that she defines as "the purposeful effort by an author to represent aspects of embodiment within the text he or she is shaping" (58). That is, the author of a rhetorical text or performance is both formed by and forming based on corporeality and ancillary forms of materiality within a larger rhetorical context. Consider the image of President Franklin Delano Roosevelt sitting by a fireplace for one of his fireside chats, which might have been physically limiting but achieved his intended rhetorical effect of physical normalcy, preferring the American public to remain ignorant of the paralysis of his legs. This third category is also of significance to our undertaking—understanding the relationship between physical activity in runners and walkers in connection to their writing activity—because we will find ourselves encountering the strengths and limitations of different writers' bodies and how they use embodiment to write and shape their rhetorical texts and performances. What we must take special pains to avoid is tokenizing one writer's body as being representative of all writers' bodies. Knoblauch reminds us that our bodily differences—in terms of race, sex, gender, and disability—influence how we think, read, and write in distinctive ways from one another. What I claim to be true about my white, female, cisgender, able-bodied experiences with running can hardly stand in for my colleague's experiences running, especially when she is challenged by homophobic and racist rhetorics—sometimes on the run, literally. Or as Knoblauch points out, the biology I share with one woman runner can hardly suffice for making generalizations about all women runners. In keeping with this thinking, I avoid making generalizations to all writers about the rhetorical constraints and affordances provided by physical movement experienced by the writers who participated in my study.

Finally, I take up Knoblauch's call to work within an embodied framework not only because the conceptual parts resonate with my grounded theory findings but because this growing subfield of embodiment in writing studies requires legitimation. As evidenced in the preceding review of literature, many have ventured into this unknown terrain only to offer ideas and opinions, and too few have sought ways to rally around a central understanding of embodied writing. Knoblauch codifies a framework for analysis from which we can get a running start toward new theories.

Conclusion

The aim of this chapter was to bring into focus the constellation of scattered and disparate theories that constitute embodied writing within the field of writing studies. If we look carefully, we can see that the diverse discussions of embodied writing are in one way or another closely related. In some cases, though, these theories will be viewed as conjecture without scientific backing. While I am not inclined to agree with this stance, I do think exploring research conducted by scientists in the fields of cognitive science, neuroscience, sports psychology, and kinesiology is a worthwhile endeavor for any writer or scholar wanting to profoundly understand embodied writing. In the next chapter, I summon forth compelling studies from several fields of psychology to shed additional light on the relationship between physical activity and writing activity.

2 The First Lap: A Trek through Embodied Cognition

Many mornings, before the rest of the world stirs, I start my day's work on the pavement. I run down my favorite roads and I think about my writing.

As my feet plod along on uneven sod, my breathing deepens, and my mind works harder to focus on the divots and dips of this suburban roadside terrain. The hardened, almost fossilized mud underneath my feet has been marred by the tires of, I imagine, a familiar suspect: a college student bordering on legally intoxicated and veering just far enough off course to leave a mark no one would care about except for me, a six-a.m. runner who's too poor to afford a headlamp that might ensure her safety as she runs at this zero-dark-thirty hour. I try to inhale and exhale through my sense of irritation, and I wonder why the city hasn't built a sidewalk here yet.

Thinking about the city reminds me that I need to pick up where I left off on my writing work from yesterday. I'm almost finished writing a piece on a Tarrant County high school that requires graduating seniors to develop capstone projects that give back to the community. It's a feel-good piece that was easy to write, but I'm struggling to come up with material for the lede. There's nothing especially cute or clever about this story. I turn over line after line in my head:

> It's back-to-school time, which means it's back-to-do-good time for one local high school. . . . [No, too hokey for this sort of human interest piece.]
>
> The last thing on most high school students' minds as they approach their senior year is how to give back to the community. [Oh, that would not be well received, would it? Don't want to hurt parents with the truth too much.]

>Next week, thousands of high school seniors across North Texas begin the last year of their secondary education. . . . [Too wordy. Maybe an anecdotal lede is good enough for this one.]

>Next week, thousands of high school seniors in the DFW area head back to their high school campuses. Some already show signs of senioritis, but some Frontier High School students are showing signs of altruism . . . [Maybe I need more of a bee-hive metaphor to be visualized. Maybe swarm is a good word to use.]

My legs shoot forward, one after the other at a forty-degree angle, with relative ease now as I find a wide shoulder of faded blacktop. Hard-raked asphalt is more pleasant to pound after a few minutes spent sinking into a semi-hardened mud-grass carpeting. My mind wants to wonder now that my legs feel strong. I'm tempted to time my steps to the tune of the soundtrack playing in my ears, Meghan Trainor's "All about That Bass." How can she say she's not a fan of treble music when she can sing soprano notes? This is not focus. Back to the writing.

I tweak this lede a little more. I make myself commit to remembering key words and parts of its construction: on Monday, thousands swarm, balancing, senioritis. I try to repeat the lede from start-to-finish again. I lose a little bit of the ending I've created. I try again. Maybe it's better now:

>On Monday, thousands of high school seniors in the DFW area will swarm back to their high school campuses. One last time, they'll try to get in the groove of balancing academic demands with extracurricular activities. Some already show signs of senioritis, but some Frontier High School students are showing signs of altruism . . .

Now I'm rounding the turns of Bluebonnet Circle, almost a mile from the house I'm renting with two fellow graduate students. I live about a mile south of my current campus home, Texas Christian University (TCU), where I study as a doctoral student in the TCU English Department. The distance from my front door to the neighborhood just above TCU's northern perimeter, where I'll end my run, is about one and three-quarter miles, making for a three and a half-mile roundtrip. These runs are starting to feel harder. My work as a student, as a graduate instructor of English composition, and my freelancing side hustle keeps me up late at night and waking earlier in the mornings than I'm used to.

Despite the adrenal fatigue I feel, I never give up my morning runs. Sometimes I supplement them with a Jillian Michaels's DVD workout, which I do in my cold, dark garage to avoid waking my roommates earlier than they'd prefer. But looking up at my laptop balancing precariously on the washer-dryer setup, under a single fluorescent strip light we have to illuminate this windowless cave, I feel uninspired. This sort of cross training is good for improving my running, I know, but I cannot think as effortlessly about my writing as I can on a run. Even with a familiar song coming from my earbuds, I have a better time thinking about my writing when I'm running. As my body moves forward, so do my thoughts. I don't feel caged, not even when self-directed imperatives to brainstorm creative content are at play. I enjoy doing the writing in my head with feet on the ground in motion. There's something wholly satisfying about moving freely through space, heart pounding, sweat beading at the edges of my hairline, mind racing with ideas for my writing that day.

Maybe this is because I know that, once I get back to my front door, I'll have a quick stretch, an even quicker shower and race to get ready. By the time I step into my office, I'll see friends in the parking lot who will want to chat, students or more friends dropping in to catch up during my office hours, and then I'll politely but frantically fumble around with my already prepared lesson plans before teaching. I might steal an hour of time later in the day to write on campus in our shared graduate student office, but social hour runneth on high in the afternoon. I could go home for a bit before my night class begins, but there I find more distraction in the form of cleaning, snacking, and virtual window shopping. I stay on campus. I fight for more writing time in subtle passive-aggressive but accepted ways, such as putting earbuds in. Even so, people find me. I give up on my hopes of doing substantial work on my writing for that day.

I manage to remember the lede I worked on this morning, entering it into my working draft I've started in Google Docs. The piece is almost finished now. I'll give it one more pass tonight.

I started and ended my day with this piece of writing, and I get the pleasure of emailing the final manuscript to my editor before I pull the chain on my bedside lamp. Prior to powering down for the night, I think for only a moment about what I want to figure out on tomorrow morning's run, but I'm too tired to set a meaningful intention. Instead, I set an alarm for 5:50 a.m., and I name this alarm: "What is your intention?"

Introduction

At numerous points in history, writers and philosophers have paused to document how movement stirs within us a desire to create. Writing icons such as Jean Jacque Rousseau, Henry David Thoreau, and Virginia Woolf have all contemplated how their daily walking habits have improved their work as writers. Louisa May Alcott, Joyce Carol Oates (to be discussed more in Chapter Four), and Jonathan Swift have all discussed the ways in which their regular running practices have benefited their more sedentary writing practices as authors. In this chapter, I begin by sharing how I became interested in the subject of embodied cognition early on in my academic career. To be clear, though, this interest formed in a recognizable way, but it took several years before I realized that I had been writing about embodied cognition all along. This chapter brings embodied cognition into fuller view and in an interdisciplinary sense, too, in that many of the definitions I have offered for consideration come to us from fields outside of composition studies.

I first became interested in embodied writing in 2012, when I was working as a graduate assistant in Iowa State University's Writing & Media Center. A writing center tutor brought a *Writing Lab Newsletter* (*WLN*) article to my attention. As part of our summer reading series, she had to choose an article for her peers to read and discuss, and the article she chose was "From Goals to Intentions: Yoga, Zen, and Our Writing Center Work," by Erika Spohrer. Due to my long history of engaging in sports and other movement practices, I was immediately intrigued by the title, and I encouraged her to facilitate that week's discussion with Spohrer's article. My nascent interest in yoga could not have prepared me for Spohrer's metaphorical comparisons between the intentions we set in yoga practice and the goals we set in writing. I was struck by Spohrer's analogy between the flexibility of the yogi's body and the writer's mind, her acknowledgment of both yoga and writing as processes, not end results. To this day, what interests me most about Spohrer's argument comes in her conclusion:

> Without a particular goal in mind, the meditator has instead a less immediate, less ego-driven intention for practices generally. Whereas a goal, focused on the short-term, would drive an

individual session, an intention takes a longer view, envisioning all of our acts as moving us slowly in a certain direction. This longer-term, more patient notion of intention makes zazen an on-going practice, a path of lifelong travel rather than a door-way of immediate entry. (12)[8]

I know this analogy to be true of my own yoga practice and certainly of my daily writing practice. My usual inclination in a yoga class is to stretch deeply into a pose—due in part to hypermobility in several joints—and to attack longer writing projects with long binge writing sessions until the work is finished. My in-depth study in a yoga teacher training pro-gram, however, has changed the way I move into poses, and the many months I have spent writing this book in fifteen- or thirty-minute dai-ly intervals reflects a newfound willingness to focus on "more patient notion[s] of intention" I have come to know through yoga. I began using this analogy to explain the writing process to my writing students the following fall semester. It was not until I proposed to teach "English 10803T: Yoga-Zen Writing," a themed first-year writing (FYW) course I developed at Texas Christian University, that I had an opportunity to explore what writing scholars have written about the role of the mind-body connection in teaching. Having spent several years researching this connection, I understand now that the separation of mind from body is an artificial division of the human experience in most all known areas of study, not just writing and writing psychology research.[9] In 2012, however, I began researching within the field of composition studies to uncover past research on writing in connection to bodily practices. My research took me down a series of winding trails, revealing that our field has not sufficiently explored this important relationship between writing activity and physical activity.

THE BRAIN ON EXERCISE

Depending on the intended cognitive outcome, different brain struc-tures play different roles in the grand performance of an embodied cog-nition act. Likewise, different forms of exercise that have been studied demonstrate that the type of movement can have dramatic effects on memory and learning. Without going into an overwhelming amount of detail, a few of those brain structures are worth elaborating.

In the 1990s, neurophysiologists discovered that the cognitive abil-ity to write is regulated by the cerebellum, a section of the brain resting below the four main lobes and on top of the brain stem (Hallett and Grafman 297). Long thought to have been central to movement and balance control, this structure still is not widely associated with the writing process. Unlike the Broca's area—which is given ample credit for the development of writing—the cerebellum is now thought to play a key role in the act of writing in addition to the maintenance of gross motor skills. Additionally, by assisting in making neural connections between the left and right hemispheres, the cerebellum supports both expressive and motor activities (Hallett and Grafman 297). Another structure, the hippocampus, is a bulb-like structure squeezed between the brainstem and the amygdala, and its central function pertains to memory-making. Interestingly, the size of the hippocampal region has been linked to a person's ability to retain memory, with shrinkage occurring in later adulthood when memory tends to decline (Erickson et al. 3017). To guard against shrinkage and protect memory, a group of psychology researchers ran a randomized clinical trial to test whether or not aerobic exercise in the form of walking might prevent memory loss. The research team divided 120 sedentary older adults (ages fifty-five to eighty) into two groups: sixty in a group for stretching and sixty in a group for walking. After one year of either stretching or walking each week, the team found that the walking group was able to reverse measured decline in their hippocampal volume and reported better memory function as a result (Erickson et al. 3022). Likewise, elderly participants who exercised on stationary bikes until an aerobic effect was measured retroactively enhanced their memories (Segal 1011). These findings suggest the exceptional effect exercise can have on neuroplasticity, or the shaping of the brain, later in life (Voss et al. 32). Elderly individuals engaging in aerobic exercise might have a cognitive edge over their peers who avoid exercise, but what about those partaking in other forms of fitness? When compared to resistance training and balance-toning exercises, aerobic walking far surpasses these other forms of exercise in improving memory retention (Nagamatsu 1).

Similarly, electrophysiological changes in the brain take place not long after runners take their first few strides out the door. In a 2011 study, neuroscientific researchers tracked the electrophysiological signals flowing through the brains of runners, finding that as running speed increased so did the rate at which runners generated gamma waves in the brain (Oaten and Cheng 717). Gamma waves are associated with "cognitive functions, including attention, learning, temporal binding, and awareness," leading researchers to hypothesize that the increase in gamma waves in running and in cognitive activities is the result of the brain preparing to adapt to a new environment that requires learning a different pattern of movement or thinking (Oaten and Chen 717). If a writer says that she can engage with writing at various stages of cognitive function while running—be it writing, editing, or memorizing writing—it is possible that she is producing gamma waves associated with both running and writing activity. What if all writers who run were aware of this possibility? Increased awareness of how these gamma waves work could encourage writers to engage in more physical activities to the benefit of their writing.

The effects of exercise on cognitive function have been observed in school-age children—although greater interest in learning rather than memory has driven these studies. In one such experiment, two psychologists tested to see whether just twelve minutes of aerobic activity might improve the selective attention of sixth- and seventh-grade students. This spurt of exercise as intervention, though brief, had a notable impact and has since been discussed as a promising intervention (Tine and Butler).

Too few primary and secondary educational programs have tapped into the potential of the mind-body relationship in writing, but there are a handful of exemplary programs willing to navigate what the relationship between writing activity and physical activity looks like for younger students. One such program in the United Kingdom is called Move4words. Labeled as a creative intervention, Move4words crafted curriculum inspired by embodied cognition theories, and then ran trials on 348 students aged seven to thirteen years (McClelland 83). In each of the three "pilot-controlled trials," the students engaged in daily activity sessions for twelve weeks, and the type of activity presented a graduated advancement in terms of difficulty that progressed over the twelve-week period and included mild aerobic exercises to develop visual attention, mental concentration, arm- and leg-movement coordination, and relaxation techniques (McClelland 87). The majority of student participants demonstrated improvement in academic writing performance with the greatest gains seen in those performing in the bottom fifth of their classes before the trials began (McClelland 83). From cognitive science research, the field of composition studies receives confirmation that our biology and physiology can benefit our writing activity. Embodied cognition builds on neuroscientific findings to build a sturdier foundation for itself as a growing area of psychological study.

Later, in 2016, Harvard School of Education researcher Elisabeth Osgood-Campbell co-developed a Mind, Brain, and Education Program for use in general education curricula in secondary schools that pulls from embodied cognition research to unite intellectual and physical pursuits. Osgood-Campbell has been quick to acknowledge the mind-body disconnect that defines our contemporary education paradigm. In a journal by the same title of the program, Osgood-Campbell names the problem of disembodiment that is plaguing the current educational paradigm:

> The dominant approach to learning as a purely mental activity shapes expectations of [writer] behavior. . . . Many administrators believe that to increase test scores, more time must be spent on the academic skills of reading, writing, and mathematics at the expense of other education activities. Thus, many have reduced or eliminated physical education and/or recess periods to gain more instructional time. (3)

Children as they learn to write are possibly given more time to develop writing skills and less time to develop physical awareness, which may be to the detriment of their writing development (3). Osgood-Campbell goes on to cite several neuroscientific studies that substantiate her claim that the dominant educational paradigm's increased focus on literate learning over physical education classes may be of detriment to young learners.

At any age, enhanced learning and memory may be brought on through consistent exercise practices. Physical fitness supplements the development of structures in the brain that are central to learning and memory, both skills being closely tied to the ability to write well. Although memory may invoke past experiences with memorization techniques for tests, I am referring to memory's relationship with rhetoric and writing practice. More specifically, memory is one of five canons of rhetoric and composition set forth in Cicero's *De Inventione*. All of these findings from cognitive and sports psychologists should be considered as we move from this concrete discussion of anatomical structures to a more abstract though equally pertinent discussion of embodied cognition in the next section.

DEFINING EMBODIED COGNITION

Every discipline—from composition studies to kinesiology—defines the term a little differently. In this section, I discuss notable definitions before adopting the definition of embodied cognition I use for the rest of the book.

Previously, I explained composition scholars Charles Bazerman and Howard Tinberg's succinct, writing-focused definition of embodied cognition, which was that "embodied cognition draws in addition upon the physical and affective aspects of the composing process," noting the attention to affective or emotional feeling (74). I have also explored how other composition scholars have variously described what embodied cognition could be before the term became ubiquitous. Long before composition studies was even legitimized as a field of study, Maria Montessori advanced detailed claims about this concept.

As an Italian scientist in the 1930s, Montessori took a keen interest in explaining and defining the creative capacities of young children. Montessori claimed that creatively gifted children possess a strong *inner orientation* described as a "muscular sense which enables an individual to become aware of the different positions taken by the various parts of his body and which requires a special kind of memory, the 'muscular memory'" (56). One "indispensable factor" in the development of this creative sense is movement or "physical activity," through which learners "come in contact with external reality, and it is through these contacts that we eventually acquire even abstract ideas" (Montessori 97). In explaining the significance of movement in relation to learning generally, Montessori gives the example of handwriting, which, she claims, engages "mind and hand" at once to satisfy a "vital instinct" to do work and learn the work of writing through the physical movement of pen in hand. When rhythm and repetition from handwriting are practiced, this physical movement supports the intellectual work of young writers with the powerful senses of satisfaction and restfulness that follow (131, 120). An act of penmanship displays embodied cognition's connection to a writing process in a literal way. By handwriting, a writer's hand takes to motion as her thoughts take form on the page.

A compelling cross-disciplinary definition comes from *The Embodied Mind*, a book co-authored by two cognitive psychologists and a philosopher:

> By using the term embodied we mean to highlight two points: first that cognition depends upon the kinds of experience that come from having a body with various sensorimotor capacities, and second, that these individual sensorimotor capacities are themselves embedded in a more encompassing biological, psychological and cultural context. (Varela et al. 172–73)

Naturally, composition scholars might read the term "embodied cognition" and immediately think of the cognitivist research that faded out of focus several decades ago, but embodied cognition is not to be confused with cognitivist approaches to studying writing. Unlike the cognitive theories of writing pioneered by noted compositionist Linda Flower and psychology researcher John R. Hayes, this new attention to the mind counts the body as one of the most integral factors influencing the mind's processes. Therefore, the mind is not necessarily separate from the body. Rather than apply generalist, brain-oriented theories to any writer, the embodied mind situates a writer in a particular sensorimotor context. As Knoblauch emphasizes in "Bodies of Knowledge," the sensory experience of a body that can feel, smell, hear, taste, and see varies widely from body-to-body, and in turn, equally as many variances are likely to occur in regard to our motor capacities, which are experienced in situated contexts. To the second point made by Varela et al., then, all of our sensorimotor experiences affect the body and mind as we move and think.

Gathering from the many contending definitions of embodied cognition, I want to offer one more definition that we might reckon with. In the context of writing, I define embodied cognition as the process by which we attune ourselves to the sensorimotor and affective capacities we have to engage in physical movement and to contemplate corporeal sensation for the purpose of writing. My research seeks to understand how embodied cognition can maximize the writing processes of professional writers through reflection on our sensorimotor and affective experiences as well as holding firmly to an interest in what these findings mean for the teaching and learning of writing. Therefore, I operate from an interested stance of paying attention to what embodied cognition holds for students of writing. In the next section, we take another graduated step forward by looking into the six views of embodied cognition, a layer of graduated complexity that offers us a nuanced understanding of how acts of embodied cognition can be used by the brain differently.

Six Views of Embodied Cognition

For what purposes can we envision embodied cognition? By 2002, psychological researcher Margaret Wilson classified six claims of embodied cognition, or views as she calls them. In her field these views are seen as fundamental and common ways of thinking, ways that include mental imagery, episodic memory, implicit memory, reasoning, and problem-solving (Wilson 633–34). Each of the six views may be applied to the cases featured later in this study. Worth noting, however, is that some of these views are distinctly more pertinent to the analysis of participants' embodied cognition experiences. The six views of embodied cognition are as follows:

1.   Cognitive processes are situated, varying depending on the real-world contexts in which they are carried out;

2.   cognitive processes must be understood with respect to the specific temporal constraints imposed on our brains by the environment when cognitive tasks are carried out;

3.   cognitive processes recruit the material, symbolic and social structure of the environment, *reducing* what actually needs to be performed in the mind itself;

4.   cognitive systems can be viewed as extended, where there is no sharp divide between internal and external contributions to cognition;

5.   the function of cognition is not primarily to represent the external world but to guide action in it and

6.   even cognition that takes place in the 'mind' proper relies on knowledge structures that emerge from body-based experiences. (Wilson 625)

Reading these views of embodied cognition, one can imagine the ways in which these claims define how physical activity supports the cognitive load that writing entails.

The *first view* denotes the situatedness of a task with specific inputs and outputs affecting the cognitive act. The perception and action of the activity are shaped by "the context of a real-world environment," so scholars should analyze the effects of this environment on cognition

(Wilson 626). In this view, the physical and material circumstances surrounding embodied cognition determine the outcome. A cold and stinging rain might make thinking about one's writing project for the day nearly impossible. Or idyllic weather conditions accompanied by a good night's sleep and new running shoes might make for one of the most memorably pleasant runs of one's life, a run so good you have to write about it later. Embodied cognition has a hand, so to speak, in the cognitive processing of a running experience in connection to one's creative thinking and perhaps later writing about that run.[10]

The *second view* accounts for the effects of time that may help or hinder an embodied cognition experience in a way that places pressure on actors because awareness of time more frequently pressures actors to make decisions about movement. Timelessness would likely not apply pressure to actors, but most cognitive acts we tackle are time sensitive in one way or another. The time it takes to set a personal record for speed or distance impacts how creatively or generatively one can think when running. If the rate of physical exertion is too high, the runner might not be able to engage in thinking about her writing process on the run.

The *third view* touches on a process by which writers find relief from the intellectual weight of a deeply cognitive writing task by employing sensorimotor activities that release mental tension and restore the mind for future writing tasks. In Wilson's words, "we exploit the environment to reduce the cognitive workload" (626). For example, a writer could run in an environment, outdoors or indoors, that feels removed from the writing task, providing the writer space to distance oneself from the work and unwind after a challenging cognitive session. For this third view, engaging in embodied cognition feels restorative.

In the *fourth view*, what is meant by a system is left rather open-ended, but Wilson succinctly states that any cognitive system is an organization that is open to and influenced by other minds, bodies, and elements—more like the situatedness of an environment than the situatedness of a task described in the first view. In this claim, the "information flow between mind and world is so dense and continuous that . . . the mind alone is not a meaningful unit of analysis" (626). The system can also be thought of as a closed circuit through which energy flows, but if the mind or the environment cease to affect one another, this claim about embodied cognition cannot be fully realized. In writing studies, we know that systemic functional approaches to teaching account for learners' past and present experiences with writing, looking at various contexts to help writers discern the systems in or for which they write. Therefore, this fourth claim easily undergirds pre-existing pedagogical findings.

The *fifth view* speaks to the role of an embodied cognition act as a means of guiding action as opposed to representation. This view addresses navigating spatial-object orientation within one's "system of vision" (Wilson 632). Or, in other words, the way our eyes intake visual-sensory-physical information communicates to our minds the functional relevance of any object within our line of sight. Wilson gives the example of a sunset being more difficult to interact with in terms of embodied cognition because the sun is so far off in the distance that its positioning does have as much of an immediate impact on us as, say, a car moving toward us at thirty miles per hour. This view's relevance to sensory processing of the physical is pertinent. Surely, we can imagine the ways in which our processing of material objects in front of us and in our periphery might disrupt or alter our movement patterns while running. The same is true for writing. If the size of the typeface I am using to compose is too small, I might lean in, fully engaging the weakness of my spine caused by "text-neck" and past engagements with composing technologies that have a functional relevance to my body and may limit or impact my cognitive processing of what I am writing about. The writing might not flow as freely as it would if I were, say, seeing the text in a larger size and having to strain less to see. My MacBook Air in front of me, the words framed on a thin screen, and their physical size of those words guide the actions I take as I compose.

Finally, the *sixth view* carries the term knowledge structures, which is an embodied cognition strategy used by writers who rely on the mind's "body-based experiences," and then translates those experiences into new ways of thinking about writing. Wilson gives the example of a person counting fingers to make a cognitive task easier to process (633). When thinking about the expression, "It's a marathon, not a sprint." we know that most people will not run or walk a marathon's distance in their lifetimes, not all at once anyway. Personally, I have not run a marathon. While I hope to attempt this great distance one day, I do not need to have trekked on foot for a marathon's worth of consecutive miles to partially understand this expression. I, or anyone else for that matter, can imagine that the physical exertion I feel when sprinting or moving quickly through time and space in a physical sense might mirror how I engage in other activities, such as writing.

A sprint of writing to me occurs when I have twenty minutes to sit in my car between off-campus dual credit instructor observations and I choose to stop-drop-and-write for that short stretch rather than respond to email from my phone. A marathon of a writing experience might feel more like a spring break retreat into my office with lights off, shades drawn, research clips and piles of coding data spread everywhere before I start binge writing. When I use the expression "It's a marathon, not a sprint." to describe my plans for writing, I imagine that the physical discomfort and mental fatigue one feels after running a marathon is akin to the achiness and exhaustion I feel after a day spent writing. Of course, the two are not one and the same; running requires more physical exertion, to be sure. But understanding one abets action and approach in the other when the body is, as Wilson says, "off-line" or not moving quickly or strenuously (626).

CONCLUSION

Great possibility for theorizing in composition studies lies in each of these six views, especially for writers seeking to understand the embodied nature of writing. I will reference and return to these claims throughout this book, especially the third and sixth views, which have informed the theoretical concepts of generative thinking, restorative thinking, and knowledge structuring that I define in the next chapter. As I move forward, I will gesture back to these concepts frequently as I use them to explicate the amply embodied language choices of well-known authors Joyce Carol Oates, Haruki Murakami, and Dr. George Sheehan.

3 In the Zone: Research on Walking and Running

"Nun-nun-nun-nun! Nunnnn!" hollers my one-, almost two-year-old toddler as he runs around a splash pad just south of our home in Denton, Texas. I wince with a breathless smile as he punches his right fist up and down as if he's driving his own self-propelled stick shift; his arm always assumes this motion when he runs excitedly.

Around this time last year, he realized he could wobble on two stick-like legs that jutted out cautiously in front of him as his arms reached out to surrounding air for balance. Now I watch as his chubby, rounded knees pop forward. I study how each knee barely bends but flutters forward fast enough to be almost imperceptible. With legs firing like tiny pistons on the crumb rubber padding beneath his feet, he's laughing maniacally as the water spouts splash his open mouth, pleased with himself for finding this new ability to move faster than he's ever moved before. Little blond cowlicks have been wet and matted to his forehead, making for rivulets of spring water running into his eyes. He wipes at them without stopping to stand still until he trips over his grey Native slip-on shoes. Within seconds, he's up and running again, giggling at either his misstep or the ego that drives him forward. I am unsure.

It's so hot in Texas in August that I can see the heat rising off the ground. I'm also seven months pregnant with my second child, so the wall of heat bakes my body from the outside in. I'm too tired and too heavy to jump off my beach towel and run around with him, but this doesn't deter all thirty-two inches of him lighting up with joy as he runs freely through a splash pad sprinkler, I applaud his "running," which looks more like the Olympic event of racewalking. His feet barely leave solid ground; most of his energy is misdirected into the clenching of two tiny fists full of enthusiasm.

For him, running makes everything more fun. If we need to throw away a dirty diaper, we run to do it. If we go to play outside, he runs out of the open garage door faster than I can finish saying, "Stay where mama can see you!" I marvel at the possibility of him loving running as much as I do. Maybe one day. My friend Tanesa's son runs with her some evenings, and I wonder if my son, who will likely tower over me by the end of high school, will want to run with his mother at some point. Will I even be in good enough shape to continue running in a decade? Will this pregnancy result in another C-section surgery that requires me to stop running for a while? And if so, will I be met again with terrible nerve pain at a healing incision site?

In my first pregnancy, I stopped running in week thirty-four, but I never stopped walking. In this second pregnancy, I stopped running just yesterday. Now in week thirty, my hips ache and pop more than they did the first time around, and the eighty-degree morning temperatures have drained what was left of my motivation. My running is in a season of drought. My inspiration to write is shrinking faster than the expansive clay earth that buckles the concrete of local roads. Morning and evening walks will tide me over with enough mental release for now.

But my toddler does not understand why I must slow down. Our morning jaunts through the neighborhood—with him strapped into the hunter green jogging stroller and me pushing from behind—leave something to be desired for him. Or as he says, "Le-go faaass!"

First, we walk; then we run. And then, for reasons often related to age, employment, or our bodies, we return to walking.

INTRODUCTION

Any form of forward motion exists on a continuum—a spectrum of movement that cannot be mapped universally but must be plotted individually. What some call running, others call jogging. What some call jogging looks more like walking to the unfeeling, removed observer.[11] When I drive to the south branch of my local library, I spend a good half mile or so driving along the perimeter of South Lakes Park, which has a very visible walking-running-cycling trail on the edge nearest the road. I watch people walking their dogs at a leisurely pace or a runner heel-striking the concrete with impressive velocity. My favorite sighting, however, is the runner who does not look like they are running. I do not mean for that statement to sound demeaning in any way. In fact, I imagine that my running looks more like labored walking, especially when struggling to make my way up some of the hills or false flats of my neighborhood roads. My fair share of unflattering race photos also assures me that my running form, although deemed good in past consultations with experts, hardly embodies a long-legged, gazelle-like prance that I imagine I look like when the running feels good (usually by the finish of mile one or when coasting downhill). I love surveying this trail for runners' forms because I love to think about where they are on their personal movement spectrum. Look closely enough at a runner in motion's face and you will see measured pain or an enviable level of physical exultation. Does the running appear to be hurting them? Are they wincing? Are they lip-syncing almost indiscernibly to whatever is on their iPhone? Does their form look relaxed or pained? How tightly have they wrapped fingers around thumbs or are their arms relaxed at their sides? While there's no way to be sure what a person is thinking or feeling while running, you can watch and perceive. If people feel like they are running, they tend to wear signs of running all over their bodies. There is no one way to define what running looks like for everyone, though, because the speed or intensity at which one runs will vary too greatly from person-to-person.

As I shared in my introductory narrative to this chapter, too, we walk or run for different reasons throughout our days and our seasons of life. Running is often thought to be an elevated level of walking because we learn to walk before we learn to run, albeit some parents take exception by claiming their children learned to run first. Regardless of our reasons for engaging in one form of forward motion over another, I find it helpful to understand some of the science behind the mechanics and the psychology of walking and running. I want to acknowledge that there are other forms of forward motion I will not focus on in this chapter not because those forms of motion are not valid or meaningful to the creative experience, and I recognize that running and walking are able-bodied actions that are not available to all. In Chapter Seven, I will discuss in more detail ways to make forward motion accessible to all bodies and why that is important based on what I learned from teaching embodied ways of being in the writing classroom. The focus on walking and running in this chapter is to frame what my professional and student writing participants showed me, which was that walking and running are two forms of physical movement that are especially generative and restorative when engaging in the creative process of writing.

Walking

More widely known than the creative benefits to writing are the physical and mental health benefits of walking. Peeling ourselves away from our desks to take a walk feels difficult at times, but when we do, we give our minds permission to ease up on a writing session that has become too difficult. Sometimes, under the most fortunate of circumstances, what we release in terms of writing stress comes back to us in terms of writing creativity. In his book, *In Praise of Walking*, Shane O'Mara spotlights this taken-for-granted ability so many people possess and that some of the world's most renowned thinkers have held onto since ancient times.[12] He emphasizes how walking strengthens our bodies, increases blood flow to our brains, and can actually help our brains grow in a way that improves learning and memory (10–11). If walking weren't already enough of a physical and mental commodity to our health and well-being, this type of movement is almost medicinal for our cells, or a "balm for body and brain," as O'Mara says. Both walking and running increase our brain's production of a molecule known as brain-derived neurotrophic factor (BDNF) which experts liken to "molecular fertilizer produced within the brain, because it supports structural remodeling and growth of synapses after learning" (137).[13] Imagine how these benefits would improve the health of a writer. How might she write more clearly or be more exacting in her prose descriptions than if she were experiencing poorer health? How might she connect better with her audience? Or, and most importantly, how might she feel better about the writing she has created in a healthy state of mind and movement—as opposed to feeling tired, rundown, or even paralyzed by the stagnancy of a desk-bound lifestyle?

Walking is a complex cognitive endeavor, so it is worth breaking down into parts of mechanical motion. O'Mara helps us visualize the micro-movement patterns required to walk:

> During walking, one foot always remains on the ground, unlike running, where both feet can leave the ground simultaneously. Walking is the outcome of an extraordinary collaboration between top-down control by the brain, bottom-up input from the feet and legs, and a mid-level rhythmical control system based in the spinal cord that functions as a 'central pattern generator' (CPG). (73)

Being a biped takes greater bodily intelligence than most of us realize. Bodily intelligence can be thought of as the taken-for-granted ways in which our minds orchestrate our movement patterns to our benefit with little to no active thinking required on the part of the mover. As O'Mara describes, sensory input from the brain, the feet, and the spinal cord work in harmony to coordinate our ability to walk effortlessly to any place we like. The science of walking, then, is something to be mastered.

Where one walks is as powerful a determinant of one's creative experience. In one study, walking outside at an arboretum was shown to have a positive effect on walkers' individual memories (Berman et al.). In another longer study, or series of experiments, conducted by experimental psychologists at Stanford University in 2014, it was seen that not only does "walking [boost] creative ideation in real time and shortly after" but that walking outside produced "the most novel and highest quality analogies" in contrast to other walking simulations, including walking inside, on a treadmill inside, or being pushed in a wheelchair outside (Oppezzo and Schwartz 1142). Also very interestingly, walkers reported experiencing a residual creative boost directly after a walking session when they took their seats (Oppezzo and Schwartz 1142). The results of this Stanford study were picked up by numerous media outlets, giving intellectual capital to several writers who saw a relationship between writing activity and physical activity, including *The New Yorker* writer Ferris Jabr. In that same year, Jabr composed a think piece-style essay that drew conclusions about the benefits of walking to writers but opposed the idea that running can benefit writers. After interviewing lead researcher M. Oppezzo, Jabr staked his own interesting claim: "Walking at our own pace creates an unadulterated feedback loop between the rhythm of our bodies and our mental state that we cannot experience as easily when we're jogging at the gym, steering a car, biking, or during any other kind of locomotion." Although this may be Jabr's experience, it has not been my experience nor has it been the experience of all embodied writers. Jogging, or running, can be useful to some writers who are able to think about their writing while on the run.

Running

Running is the next physical progression to be taken after one has mastered, or at least become interested in exceeding, the pace at which one can walk. Though not always explicitly stated, running is often put on a pedestal that walking cannot quite amble up to. In footraces, speed is prized. Monetary awards and sponsorships are presented to top race finishers who outpace their peers in half and full marathon competitions.

Taking a break to walk in any distance of race—be it a 5K, 10K, or a full marathon—might be the soundest option when fatigue, cramps, or foot pain creep up, but not for a race participant who aims to win. With this distinction in mind, we can think of running as the more competitive, almost capitalistic cousin of walking. That is not to suggest that the act of running is marred with unsavory ethical underpinnings, but the growing fanfare around running has altered the way most contemporary exercisers value the miles attained through one activity over another.

American interest and participation in running races is a relatively recent phenomenon. Shelly McKenzie has written extensively on the rise of fitness culture in America since the mid-twentieth century, citing running as one of the most impactful changes to our cultural landscape. What started as a jogging movement, a way to offset American weight gain in a post-World War II era, earned the more impressive semantic of running in the 1970s as interest in the marathon event took off. Sponsored in many cases by the more affluent members of society, hobbiest runners went winding down the streets, parks, and neighborhoods mapped out by suburban sprawl, sporting their new running shoes as a badge of honor. McKenzie goes so far as to claim that physically fit bodies, especially running bodies, "became a new form of physical capital" (8). A line was drawn between the haves and the have nots:

> Fitness had become more than just a matter of health mainte-
> nance. . . . Maintaining a regular workout routine became a
> demonstration of one's interior mettle. And if being an exerciser
> somehow made you a better person, it followed that people who
> didn't work out (or at least looked like they didn't) were lazy,
> unmotivated, and undisciplined. (7)

Somewhat out of necessity with the rise in heart attacks, white Protestant males of the greatest generation (those born in the first three decades of the twentieth-century) were among the first to propel the sport of running into public limelight (McKenzie 125). White women soon followed but more to fulfill cosmetic intentions, and they were severely limited in terms of how they could participate in the sport publicly. The iconic image of Katherine Switzer, the first woman to register for and run the Boston Marathon in 1967, comes to mind. Switzer, who nearly passed for male in a sea of men for several miles thanks to a loose-fitting crew-neck sweater and joggers, was soon chased down by race organizer Jock Semple. In an ironic turning of the tide, women registrants now exceed male registrants in American foot races of almost every distance—5K, 10K, and half marathon—with the exception of the marathon (fifty-four percent of male registrants versus forty-six percent of female registrants) (*Running USA Report 2020*).

Even if Americans are walking more on a daily basis, from their car to their office or around the corner to the grocery store, we have more information on who, when, and how far Americans are running. Whereas walking is a more physically accessible, slower-paced alternative to running, more data is available on the latter thanks to annual reports generated by Running USA, a not-for-profit organization that tracks American interest and participation in running races. In the *2020 Running Trends Report*, Running USA documented that 17.62 million Americans registered for a foot race of a 5K distance or greater in 2019, down only slightly from 18.1 million in 2018 but no less impressive. Across genders, the average age of registrants was thirty-eight years old and the most popular season for sanctioned running events is spring (with thirty-five percent of 2019 races occurring in spring months), followed by fall (thirty-one percent), summer (twenty-two percent) and in last winter (twelve percent) (*2020 Running Trends Report*).

Diversity and Safety Issues

Missing from recent running demographic reports is a more accurate snapshot of the diversity of runners in North America. The *2020 Running Trends Report* distributed information on the age and gender identities as well as the seasons and distances of race length that these individuals run, but from that report we know nothing of the race, sexual orientation, class, or other intersectional identity markers of these participants. A 2011 article in *Runner's World*, titled "Why Is Running So White?" reports that this leading organization did collect information on race in one of two biannual surveys released for that year (Jennings). When I realized this gap in existing knowledge, I contacted Running USA to see if more identity information was available than what was published in the 2020 report. The organization, which had appointed a new all-female staff in late 2020, could not comment on why race had been considered in previous surveys but not represented in the published 2020 findings. However, the research team was in the process of collecting new data on the embodied experiences of runners, asking questions pertaining specifically to issues of systemic racism, diversity and inclusion efforts within the sport, and interest in social justice-oriented event initiatives.

Questions regarding gender provided the option to select from a menu of "Female," "Male," "Gender non-binary," or "I choose not to answer." One question asked if participants cared to share their sexual orientation and another following that one asked if participants identified as transgender or not. At the halfway point in this survey, the administrators provide a comment box, above which the following prompt appears: "So that we can share your feedback with event organizers, what steps would you like to see the running industry take to promote diversity, equity, and inclusion?" The fact that these questions were featured in the most recent iteration of this survey signals promise and interest in diversity and inclusion efforts, but the presence of these questions does not directly address the existence of larger systemic issues of racism and other prejudices faced by runners around the world.

If social activism efforts have shown us anything over the last decade, it is that not all bodies enjoy the same privileges, especially not when running or walking in public spaces. One of the most influential hashtags over the last decade, #BlackLivesMatter, has been used millions of times to expose the atrocities faced by Black people when out for a run or walk (Anderson). Case in point: in response to the killing of Ahmaud Arbery, a twenty-five-year-old Black man who was out for a jog when two white men pursued him by vehicle and fatally wounded him in South Georgia in early 2020, Natalia Mehlman Petrzela penned an opinion piece for *The New York Times* in which she cited numerous news reports revealing heinous crimes committed against Black runners in every decade from the time recreational running took off in the 1960s onward. Petrzela, who is a marathoner herself and a tenured history professor at The New School in New York City, points out that despite America's support of Black track athletes in sanctioned practices and events, Black participation in recreational running remains perilous. It would stand to reason for some that walking might be perceived as a safer alternative to running due to its slower pace, but for young Black men out walking in America this is hardly the case. In light of the deaths of Michael Brown, Trayvon Martin, Elijah McClain and far too many others, journalists and researchers are paying closer attention to the targeting of Black bodies in outdoor spaces. In one study exploring the racial biases of drivers yielding for pedestrians at crosswalks, Black pedestrians had to wait 32 percent longer than white pedestrians, and Black pedestrians were twice as likely to be passed by cars than white pedestrians (Goddard et al.). These gravely disturbing findings are compounded by the unsettling experiences of LGBTQ+ race participants, who are coming forward to share the discriminatory practices they have encountered at racing events ("What Runners Want You to Know"). The fact of the matter is that any composite sketch of a sanctioned running event will look mostly white, straight, middle-class, and able-bodied. And, to add insult to injury, a lack of diversity in body size can reinforce sizeist notions of thinness as the ideal body standard (Dutch). Running USA and *Runner's World Magazine* are two institutions making a concerted effort to better understand the challenges and inequities faced by runners who identify as being part of one or more minority groups, but much more needs to be overhauled on the part of local and national running organizations as well as research partners interested in studying the experiences of minority runners. In later chapters, I account for what I can (based on what was disclosed to me) of the embodied intersectional identities of the professional and student writers I interviewed and collected data on. I see a critical need to extend my findings beyond the hauntingly white (an expression I attribute to the work of Tammie M. Kennedy, Joyce Middleton, and Krista Ratcliffe), cis-gender, and able-bodied privilege of the North American running community, and I hope other scholars will join me in the future in pursuing research on the intersectional aspects of runner-writers' identities.

The Psychology of Running

Much like walking, the psychology of running has an invisible influence on how we think as we run and what we, as writers, can gain from connecting our running to our writing. To be clear, very limited research looks specifically at the relationship between writing and running activity, but several studies on attention give us insight into what our mind is doing while we are running. In *The Runner's Brain*, long-distance runner and psychology professor Jeff Brown surveys the various kinds of conscious thought patterns that occur while exercising. These attentional patterns, known as associative and dissociative styles of thinking, distract runners from pain, boredom, and impatience to finish running distances of various lengths. These patterns can be taught, but more often than not, runners learn these patterns on their own and choose them based on personal preferences. Association occurs when a runner focuses on the sensorimotor experience of running, whereas dissociation occurs when a runner "zones out" or mentally disengages from the sensorimotor experience of running. More specifically, there are external and internal styles of association in which the runner processes sensorimotor perceptions and thoughts related to their running; when associating externally they focus on stimuli outside of their internal performance as opposed to internal association, when they focus on personal running performance, not the performance of others (Brown 52). External association occurs when a runner focuses on running experience with attention to factors outside the body, such as processing cheers from spectators as one crosses the finish line (Brown 52). Internal association unfolds when focusing intently on personal breathing patterns, counting footfalls, monitoring heart rate levels, or any other type of physical barometer requiring one to focus attention on the task of running (Brown 53). External dissociation relies heavily on factors outside the self, ones not influencing running performance, such as counting the number of red houses on the route (Brown 53). Lastly, internal dissociation occurs when the distraction of choice involves "focus[ing] the mind inward" to redirect attention away from running performance and instead internally focus on "your problems, the past, your family, work problems, your grocery list," and to this list we can add "your writing problems" (Brown 53). Internal dissociation makes space for generative thinking by freeing up mental attention from running toward other sensations or experiences so that more attention can be directed at the generation of new ideas for writing.

Whether associative or dissociative, these attentional patterns are highly dependent on the level of exertion put forth by the runner, which might also explain why Jabr considers running incompatible with the act of thinking about writing. Research has been conducted to determine what effect perceived exertion levels may have on how runners talk to themselves while running. In 2013, one study looked at how a runner's "internal dialogue" was a byproduct of their perceived exertion (Aitchison et al.). Dissociative thinking was attainable when exertion rates were of a lower intensity, whereas higher rates of intensity necessitated increases in associative thinking (Aitchison et al.). Similar results were seen in a study of rowers in 2010, giving us good reason to believe that strenuous or fast-paced exercise of any kind, not just running, makes creative thinking about the writing process very difficult (Connolly and Janelle 195, Connolly and Tenenbaum 1123). More focus and attention need to be directed toward the body's safe and effective performance of a movement pattern executed at a faster-than-normal frequency. One such study looking into the differences among association, dissociation, and the cognitive strategy of positive self-talk during athletic performance might serve as a model for consideration. In this study, the research team found that participants were more likely to persist at running as fast as they could around a quarter-mile track for thirty minutes if they used positive self-talk and dissociation rather than association as a cognitive strategy (Weinberg et al. 25).

The studies on running and exertion discussed here seem to contradict each other in terms of outcomes, but these messages are clear: The need to dissociate at higher levels of running intensity can be helpful when completing a difficult run, but running too fast may make concentrating on ideas for writing difficult. Walking might be more conducive all around to the production of ideas for writing, but thinking about and creating writing on the run is far from impossible. Much to the contrary, some physical intensity from running might heighten creative senses while runners dissociate, leaving them space and time to play with their ideas for writing while they run.

CONCLUSION

A toddler delights in a running revelation because the ability to move faster excites their mind in indescribable ways. An adult takes a walk and comes back with new ideas for a writing project because the action of walking stimulated their creative faculties. Whether running or walking, these forms of forward movement render our minds ready to receive exhilarating insights about ourselves as embodied individuals. Often taken for granted, the complex movements of walking and running might be harnessed for what they can offer writers struggling to collect their thoughts or to write creatively and productively. The next chapter introduces terminology writers and writing scholars can use to understand embodied cognition's role in the writing process more generally, but then I will apply those concepts precisely to what three writers have said about their understanding of the relationship between running activity and writing activity.

4 The Mind Flies: An Embodied Cognition Framework for Analysis

arly on the morning of September 3, 2016, my twenty-seventh birthday, I run a steamy three-mile loop around two parks bordering my South Hills neighborhood in Fort Worth, where the line between middle- and lower-income family housing is substantially blurred. I try to relax into this run, to lower my shoulders away from my ears. It's hard to let my mind roam as freely as I'd prefer when my eyes are constantly scanning for unleashed dogs and my thoughts are consumed by last-minute considerations that need to be made for the flight to Berlin I'll board in a few hours.

This isn't my first time abroad, but it is my first time attending a Schreibaschram experience, a writing retreat hosted by faculty at the Berlin Summer University of the Arts. In German, "schreib" means "write." In Hindu, "ashram" means "place of endeavor," and many dedicated yoga practitioners make pilgrimages to ancient ashram spaces in India where yoga has been practiced for thousands of years. The Schreibaschram outside of Berlin offers professional writers, doctoral, and post-doctoral students a monastic-style retreat in the Northern German countryside, where the community adheres to a strict schedule that begins every day with an hour of physical exercise, a communal breakfast, two morning writing sessions, lunch in silence, an afternoon workshop presentation on writing that incorporates mindful movement, an afternoon writing session, a communal dinner, free time spent enjoying evening walks through apple orchards or talking to other participants, and a required evening meditation session. Structured writing sessions were held in a renovated barn on the property, where fifteen desks were spaced out in tidy rows for each writer to set up their writing station as they liked—sometimes adding blankets, floor cushions, and other props to adjust bodies into more comfortable positions as the hours wore on. The Schreibaschram lasted for seven days. We were given one hour of wireless internet access a day to check in with loved ones. Cell phone use was not permitted. I feasted on the affordances of a disciplined schedule of writing, running, more writing, meditating, the soft touch of autumnal sunshine and fields of air as crisp as the apples I picked off the trees.

On the first morning of Schreibaschram, we, the uncertain participants, dotted ourselves up and down the steps outside of the red brick manor. One of our professional writing coaches, Katja Günther, let us know, first in German and then in English, that we were going for a vigorous walk. As we set off, I felt almost immediately uncomfortable in my moving body. I looked at the older women ahead of me and to my right, arms pumping, feet pounding the ground with a sense of self-assurance I wouldn't come to know before I turned thirty and had my second child. I tried to move my arms in the jaunty way they did, but I'm not the power-walking type. If I'm going to get going somewhere fast, I need to run.

After fifteen minutes, we'd arm-pumped our way to a large fork in the road. We circled up around the perimeter of this three-way stop, shifting around on what was left of the weather-worn crushed white rock, and we began a calisthenics series. Every limb spun in every direction, and the last and most curiously tantalizing callisthenic required us to "wake up our sensations" by rippling our tapping fingers up our bodies, from our toes to the crown of our heads. When this routine was complete, we were to hike back to the manor grounds for showers and breakfast. I and a few other runners asked if we could run on a little further. Katja and the other writing coach, Ingrid Scherübl, approved so long as we were able to start our writing sessions on time, and so we took off.

Every morning we ran past the clearing, we entertained different company. Our small group of runners changed based on individual need—some wanted to get back early for a shower while others were a little sore from overexerting themselves on a run the day before—but every day I kept steady company with a writing center director from Nurnberg. We talked about our personal lives—her twins, her divorce, my new marriage, and my hopes to become a mother soon—and, of course, who we were as writers—our preferences, quirks, and struggles. I produced more writing in that one week—seven days—than I have produced in many months of dedicated work—almost seventy pages of the first draft of my dissertation—and I left feeling enthused, not depleted.

Undoubtedly, being immersed in a writing-intensive refuge with fifteen deeply focused writers for a full week augmented my productivity at this retreat and led to many fascinating conversations about the relationship between physical activity and writing activity. One morning at the Schreibaschram I was eating breakfast at the far end of a long teak wood table, making conversation with three German women who were interested in my research, when Katja made a suggestion to me: "You are researching all these writers who use running to help them with their writing, but maybe for you, you could think of your writing as a new sport you must try to learn?" The conversation spiraled from there. The other two women were both avid rock climbers, and one—who was also writing a dissertation on depictions of femininity in Emersonian literature—shared with me that some of her best ideas for her writing come when she is "up there," climbing and muscling her way up the side of a cliff. From this conversation, I captured two pivotal insights. What became very clear to me through this conversation is that, for writers, the relationship between physical activity and writing activity involves embodied cognition on both ends, sometimes in a reciprocal manner, but for my interviewees, the physical activity supported the cognitive functioning of the writing activity more than the cognitive act of writing supported their participation in physical activities. Second, these women discussed their knowledge of writing processes in relation to physical movement processes but without applying formal or theoretical terms. The Emersonian critic described how her sport, rock climbing, allowed her to cognitively off-load in a way that enabled her ability to generate new ideas about writing.

I learned from living with, moving with, and writing alongside other writers in the Schreibaschram that every writer's body makes use of embodied cognition in dramatically different ways. Some writers are more aware of this phenomenon than others.

INTRODUCTION

As depicted in this chapter's opening narrative, I have felt the need to move as a writer, and this need has driven me to great lengths—physically and intellectually—to understand why I and other professional writers need movement to thrive as writers. In this chapter, I introduce readers to the world of professional writers who run, walk, or engage in acts of embodied cognition that support their work as writers. Before offering portraits of these writers, I will give a brief overview of the methods I used to conduct my research and how my findings led me to create the writing-embodied cognition terminology we need to understand why writers need to move their bodies or otherwise be attuned to the sensorimotor experiences connected to our writing processes. Namely, I explain how the writers I studied have the propensity to demonstrate tendencies of generative thinking and restorative thinking, or knowledge structuring, an embodied cognition strategy to support writing practice. By no means are these terms fixed or static. I hope that the conceptual openness of these terms will reflect the dynamic potential of physical movement in the writing process and that it does so in a way that empowers more writers to invite movement into their creative processes.

To study writing as an embodied activity requires starting by recognizing that bodies differ, and at the same time, differing bodies may share common, intersecting mental and physical experiences. Without a deeper understanding of how embodiment shapes the contexts and experiences in which writers write, we cannot begin to understand the writing process in its vastness or entirety. Given the existing gaps in our research, I sought to answer three questions. First, what is the relationship between physical activity and writing activity? Second, how can physical activity help us understand the nature of the writing process for professional academic and non-academic writers? Because of my background in teaching college writing classes (both first-year composition courses and upper-division professional writing courses), I also wanted to know how we can apply what we learn from these questions to the writing classroom. I crafted a more complex third question: Can physical activity support writing activity, especially for student writers, and if so, how? From the outset, these questions prepared me to explore physical activity as a general, catch-all phrase, one inclusive of running, walking, gymnastics, curling, or any other physical sport or practice. I knew early on that any sensorimotor experience could stoke the fires of creative, embodied writing.[14]

PROFESSIONAL WRITERS

To explore the relationship between physical activity and writing activity, I interviewed eleven professional writers who also participate regularly (more than once a week) in physical activities—defined broadly as movement that engages the body in sensorimotor and affective feeling. My participants were recruited based on whether they met two criteria: first, did they engage in current writing experience or activity that supports or defines their careers, and second, did they engage in regular physical experience or activity in any sport, performance, or personal training regimen at a professional or novice level more than once a week. With research and referrals, I was able to interview eleven writers spanning a range of writing professions and backgrounds, including eight individuals who identified themselves as academic writers two of whom preferred to think of themselves as poets—and three non-academic writers: a journalist, a novelist, and a children's book author. Although I did not intend to seek runners specifically, I was surprised to find that most of these writers engaged in running or walking as physical activity every week. Many of these participants were committed to other types of physical activity, too, including yoga, powerlifting, weightlifting, Cross-Fit training, indoor and outdoor cycling, kickboxing, and squash. Concurrently, each of the academic writers also identified as a runner at one point in their histories, with only one currently not running due to past injuries that prevented her from doing so. Six of the academic writers held tenure-track positions, three at smaller, private colleges and three at larger state universities. The two professors of literature and the one assistant professor of technical communication were marathoners. The other three enjoyed running at lower mileages, going to yoga, cycling, walking, or taking a wide variety of group exercise classes.

Why study both academic and non-academic professional writers? As a researcher, my intent has always been to understand the relationship between physical and written activity within and beyond academic institutions. I work for and teach writing at a university, but I firmly believe that not everyone learns to write in their first-year composition classes alone. Some people identify as writers as early as middle school while others fall into a job that requires them to write, soon learning they have possessed the gift of writing well for many years but not realizing their potential.

Albeit limited, there is past research that suggests academic and non-academic writers are not all that different from one another. My focus on academic and non-academic writers was inspired by the work of psychology researcher Robert Boice. In 1990, Boice published one of the first and only studies on the psychology of writing motivation. He enlisted twenty-six academic writers and twenty-six non-academic writers to "merge what writers say about writing with what researchers and scholars say in a way that helps both experienced and inexperienced writers at the writing desk" (*How Writers Journey to Comfort* xvi). Through years of data collection, Boice's work has shown that academic writers are not drastically different from non-academic writers (in the way that male writers are not strikingly different from female writers, he points out). For the purpose of understanding writing and embodied cognition across academic and non-academic contexts, I recruited both types of writers to better understand how physical activity is connected to writing activity among writers writing in different genres, with different motives.

Thus, through qualitative interviews with professional writing participants, qualitative content analysis of relevant pieces of writing those participants shared with me, and, in a few cases, the writing logs of a few participants, I coded for themes that arose from the data using a grounded theory approach to analysis.[15]

Embodied Cognition Themes

Knoblauch's embodiment framework helped identify three distinct categories: embodied language, embodied knowledge, and embodied rhetoric. By coding for embodied cognition themes in interview transcripts, writing logs, and writing samples, I can further expand the framework Knoblauch has set forth, differentiating between how embodied knowledge impacts the writer's work in generative and restorative ways as well as how embodied language assists writers in understanding their writing processes.

As defined in the previous chapter, embodied cognition is the process by which we learn how to write by attuning ourselves to the sensorimotor and affective capacities we have to engage in physical movement and to contemplate corporeal sensation. Lack of attention to the role of the body in the production of writing can be reversed to the benefit of all writers. In terms of learning, our field—and every discipline, for that matter—can apply concepts from embodied cognition to alleviate the mind-body disconnect that divests writers of opportunities to contemplate their writing in relation to their sensorimotor experiences (Osgood-Campbell 3; Rosch, Thompson and Varela 172–73). For research psychologists, embodied cognition is hardly a new theory, but this theory does present new and unfamiliar terrain to writers and writing scholars. For the latter audience, it is imperative to recall the discussion of embodied cognition claims put forth by research psychologist Margaret L. Wilson in Chapter Three. With Wilson's views of embodied cognition in mind, we can understand what embodied cognition holds for writers in terms of generative thinking and restorative thinking. In my research, knowledge structuring appeared as a theme in almost every participants' narrative. In the next section, I will discuss how I coined the term "knowledge structuring," which involves applying a knowledge structure from a physical activity onto a writing activity—an edifying action.

Themes I and II: Generative Thinking and Restorative Thinking

As an emergent pair of concepts, generative thinking and restorative thinking relate back to but expand on how embodied cognition benefits writers.[16] These are terms I developed independent of Wilson's claims of embodied cognition, but as conceptually distinct states of thinking these terms depict Wilson's ideas in more expansive, writing-relevant terms. The simplest way to distinguish generative thinking from restorative thinking is as follows: Generative thinkers are those who create new knowledge while exercising, whereas restorative thinkers are those who restore their cognitive functions while exercising.

For runners, generative thinking can happen anytime or anywhere, but especially while on a run when one thinks about their writing project by repeating new ideas, sentences, phrases, or even rethinking an organizational pattern. When the runner returns to their writing desk, the ideas generated on the run create new knowledge that supports one's writing activity. In contrast, a runner can run to avoid thinking about their writing practice with the intention of relieving the mind from a day's work spent writing; this is restorative thinking. I have often visualized restorative thinking by picturing a runner literally and metaphorically running into their sense of creativity out on a trail, away from a desk, and leaving the work of writing behind. Replace the activity of running with any other sport, and you can imagine the myriad ways that embodied cognition can occur. Yoga practitioners might flow into or away from their work. Tennis players might take shots at their writing subject with each swing of their racket, or the force of each shot might help them release the weight of the writing project they're soon to face.

The same could be said for the University of Iowa women basketball players, who came to know their writing through their athletic experiences through Julie Cheville's research. Recall that in *Minding the Body,* Cheville argues that athletic activity requires intellectual activity, calling out scholars who have dismissed athletes as an unintelligent population of writers who do little thinking on or off the court, field, or track. Without ever explicitly connecting her theory of embodied writing to embodied cognition, Cheville defines her own version of generative thinking. When practicing for or participating in athletic events or when engaging in the task of writing, Cheville claims that the athlete-writer "submit[s] him- or herself to the power of a particular way of knowing/ behaving to participate in that power, to become more effective in applying it and thus to gain the satisfaction and rewards that it offers" (64). In this example, Cheville suggests that athletes use their athletic experiences as a way of coming to understand "participat[ing] in that power," of the university and their writing classrooms. In a sense, the athletes' descriptions of thinking were generative because the athletes created new ideas for their writing, rather than using their athletic experiences to restore their minds after engaging in intense intellectual work. Cheville's writers engaged in generative thinking, seeing as how these athletes drew comparisons between their experiences as writers and athletes—thereby generating new knowledge and actively applying the knowledge structure of athletic performance to the cognitive tasks related to their writing performances.

Theme III: Knowledge Structuring

Sometimes the mind surreptitiously uses the body's knowledge to make the process of writing easier for the writer. Recall Wilson's finger counting, for example. The action of finger counting is cognitive and sensorimotor in nature in that it requires movement of one's hands and touch, and for some, Wilson says, can be acted out with highly animated efforts. On the other hand, she says, counting fingers "can also be done more subtly, differentiating positions of the fingers only enough to allow the owner of the fingers to keep track . . . like mere twitching" (632–33). Movement aids in the cognitive task of counting, so one might begin to consider "a new vista of cognitive strategies" that are also embodied (633). Such strategies might include recalling physically informed mental imagery, short- or long-term memories leaving a strong sensorimotor impression, learned skills that have been automatized, and reasoning based on past physical experiences (633–34). Wilson provides multiple definitions to elucidate the complex angles of each view. Perhaps her clearest definition of this sixth view (knowledge structuring) comes later in her article:

> Mental structures that originally evolved for perception or action appear to be co-opted and run "off-line," decoupled from

the physical inputs and outputs that were their original purpose, to assist in thinking and knowing. . . . In general, the function of these sensorimotor resources is to run a simulation of some aspect of the physical world, as a means of representing information or drawing inferences. (633)

Wilson states that knowledge structures are used every time we invoke mental imagery to aid our thinking processes or every time we tap into our episodic memory of past embodied experiences that can inform our approach to current and ongoing experience (633). If we apply such strategizing to our own challenging cognitive tasks, we have to select and apply our knowledge of a past physical experience. Effectively, we would be reading the structure of the past experience—how it began, what was challenging about it, what brought about resolution of cognitive difficulty—and applying our reading of the past structure to our reading of the current structures of the cognitive task we hope to understand better.

What embodied expressions do you hear spoken in everyday conversation? "Play it by ear." "Walk a mile in her shoes." or "Keep your chin up." If we are playing something by ear, then we are actively engaging our sense of hearing to adapt to a new situation. This familiar phrase can be used for almost any and every cognitive activity I can think of because it encourages scholars to adopt adaptation as a strategy. The phrase also requires the reader to trust a past experience of playing it by ear, thereby informing how the reader approaches a new situation. Past, present, or imagined experiences structure how one will approach the situation that lies ahead. Likewise, if we ask someone to "Walk a mile in their shoes." we ask the listener to understand the challenges of another person by briefly imagining and feeling what it would be like to be someone else, literally or metaphorically walking with the emotional or physical burdens that person carries. Such a structure elicits empathy and builds a bridge of mental connection between what a person knows about someone else and oneself, forging a new relationship between two experiences that can be structured very differently otherwise.

Knowledge structuring presents itself from time-to-time when I encounter other runners and walkers in my neighborhood. For me, there is something decidedly awkward about passing another runner or walker, so when I pass I try to wave a gentle hand signifying my friendliness, to slow down so as to not seem as though I am trying to outpace them, and to not pant so loudly as to rudely intrude on their private inner monologues. I see these moments as also being interesting opportunities to check in with my ego by placing myself in another's position. That is, when I find myself moving faster than another runner or walker, I try to avoid gloating about my speed and instead ponder the reasons as to why we are moving at different paces. For example, most mornings in the seven o'clock hour, I will cross paths with a late middle-aged Black man, who I see as being well-dressed in a driver's cap and a collared shirt and frequently FaceTiming with someone on his iPhone. At some point prior to our crossing encounter, our eyes will always meet, and we will usually gesture toward each other with a casual raising of one hand and a quick smile to acknowledge that we see each other. In this fleeting and familiar moment, I have often wondered why he chooses to walk instead of run. FaceTiming while running would be incredibly fatiguing for both him and the person he is talking to, to be sure, but perhaps he has another reason as to why he has chosen not to run. Maybe a pre-existing injury prevents him from running? Maybe he feels a weariness in his bones that I will come to know in my next decade of life? Or, maybe, being a Black man in a predominantly white suburban neighborhood, he feels unsafe breaking into a breezy sprint down one of our asphalt hills? And so, when I begin to think about the speed of other runners, like this neighbor I habitually greet, I stop and put myself in the other person's shoes. Can I try on what they might be feeling? Can I not? Does my bodily memory allow me to relate to them in a sensory way? Or am I only able to imagine what they are experiencing? With this simple thought experiment, I regularly open myself up to better understanding knowledge structuring. "Walk a mile in their shoes" is a short and sweet way of alluding to the ability to structure my understanding of another's intersectional identity experiences as an embodied mover through past, present, or imagined embodied knowledges, and to do so in a way that promotes new knowledge making.

Knowledge structures operating for the purposes of achieving embodied cognition need not be limited to everyday physical movements. The physicality of sports brings us knowledge structures with even richer historical contexts: "He wants to play hardball." "That's par for the course." "Let's level the playing field." Or "Don't sweat the small stuff." In these examples, patterns of sensorimotor behavior, feelings, and outcomes serve as reference points or have been contextualized in the stories of others in order to structure effectively the knowledge-making experience of the listener. The listener can recall a sensorimotor experience informing the expression, but if they have not experienced the sensorimotor experience defining the expression, then they can still understand the embodied experience—of playing hardball, arriving at an expectation on a golf course, or equalizing the ability of players in any sport, for example—if only partially through imagination.[17]

WRITERS ON RUNNING

Drawing on the embodied cognition themes I have shared, we can apply this new terminology to the written ponderings of several well-known writers who have published their thoughts on the relationship between physical activity and running activity. In this next section, I will investigate how authors such as Joyce Carol Oates, Haruki Murakami, and Dr. George Sheehan examine their work as writers and runners using embodied knowledge and language to bridge the divide between these complementary pursuits.

Joyce Carol Oates

Joyce Carol Oates's fans are likely already familiar with her book, *The Faith of a Writer,* which reflects on her development as a writer over time. As the author of over fifty novels along with novellas, short stories, plays, poetry, and nonfiction pieces, Oates has ample advice for the new writer, giving counsel on topics, such as where to find inspiration and where to locate one's writing studio. What few expect to encounter in her writing memoir is the chapter titled, "Running and Writing." For anyone who dislikes running, I can only imagine what a deterrent that chapter title could be. But those who both run and write, like me, it presents an irresistible invitation. With a felicitous tone, she opens this chapter by saying,

> Running! If there's any activity happier, more exhilarating, more nourishing to the imagination, I can't think what it might be. In running, the mind flies with the body; the mysterious efflorescence of language seems to pulse in the brain, in rhythm with our feet and the swinging of our arms. Ideally, the runner-who's-a-writer is running through the land- and cityscapes of her fiction, like a ghost in a real setting. (29)

To situate this quotation within our embodied cognition framework, Oates is very clearly professing running to be a generative thinking exercise. She insinuates that, for fiction writers especially, the mind and

body travel together simultaneously and harmoniously into a new creative direction. Readers who can relate will feel a sense of satisfaction
when reading her words and the acuity with which she captures their
experiences thinking about writing while running. Readers who cannot
relate are poised to imagine how running gives Oates an opportunity to
carry her ideas for fiction writing along with her and to develop them
while engaged in the act of running. Later in the chapter, she confesses
that she almost never invents ideas for her stories while at a typewriter,
but rather, she brings to the typewriter what she has invented only after
intensively crafting her ideas while running and then after having composed them in longhand form (Oates 35). She ends the chapter by saying
these "twin activities," running and writing, have kept her and so many
other writers "reasonably sane" as she has grappled with the complexity
of her craft (Oates 36). These other writers she refers to include infamous
walkers, mostly, such as Wordsworth, Coleridge, and Thoreau. Somewhat haughtily she suggests that running is far superior to walking as a
generative thinking exercise, although she is not the first to do so.

Oates's embodied philosophies become a point of interest not only
with *Atlantic* writer Nicholas Ripatrazone, who was discussed in Chapter One, but also with *New York Magazine* writer Melissa Dahl. One
year after Ripatrazone, Dahl composed her own think piece-style exposition to weave together what famous writers and scientists were saying
about running or walking's impact on writing, memory, and the creative
process (albeit in different ways). What she does differently than Ripatrazone, who again asks "Why do writers run?" is to hedge a claim that
scientists are not accounting for the significance of what she calls mind
wandering. By "mind wander" Dahl means to suggest that our cognitive
thinking enables us to internally dissociate, just as Jeffrey Brown outlined in Chapter Four, and she is correct. Scientists have been quick to
place the brain "on camera" to capture images of which lobes and structures light up when activated while running, thereby letting us draw
conservative conclusions about how physical activity switches on different neural centers. Dahl's critique of scientists points to a collective
lack of scholarly interest in studying the moment when the brain starts
to internally dissociate while running—or engaging in other forms of
sensorimotor movement. She ends her piece by providing a quotation
from internationally known writer, Haruki Murakami: "I just run. I run
in a void," he writes. "Or maybe I should put it the other way: I run
in order to *acquire* a void" (17). Murakami hypothesizes that there are

times when he runs to escape his own thinking and nothing more. His intention is not to run in order to write more creatively or productively. Rather, he just wants to run away from the trappings of his day-to-day writing work.

Haruki Murakami

Murakami, like Oates, is frequently cited on the topic of running and writing, particularly for his thoughts on how running provides opportunities for restorative thinking. His memoir, *What I Talk about When I Talk about Running*, takes Oates's thoughts about the relationship between running and writing to an entirely new level of understanding, giving a book-length treatment of the topic from his perspective as the reader tags along on several of Murakami's international running adventures. In one chapter, he is singed by the Grecian sun on his solitary trek from Athens to Marathon, and in another chapter he is humbled by a sixty-two-mile ultramarathon he dared to take in Northern Japan. In most of these places, running is, as previously stated, Murakami's void, his "cozy, homemade void," or his "nostalgic silence," and in these descriptions we see his own version of running as a source of restorative thinking, the respite he needs (23).

Equally easy to track throughout his memoir is his description of writing and running in similar terms, signaling a kind of knowledge structuring that he uses to bring the two activities closer together. He might not think about his writing while running. In fact, he claims he remembers little to nothing that he thinks about while running. Yet his likening of these activities demonstrates the synergy of the two together. He writes, "I didn't start running because somebody asked me to become a runner. Just like I didn't become a novelist because someone asked me to. One day, out of the blue, I wanted to write a novel. And one day, out of the blue, I started to run — simply because I wanted to" (Murakami 150). The juxtaposition of writing and running in his comparison could not be clearer or more direct. In a less direct but no less captivating example, Murakami shares that

> [m]ost runners run not because they want to live longer, but because they want to live life to the fullest. If you're going to while away the years, it's far better to live them with clear goals and fully alive then in a fog, and I believe running helps you to do that. Exerting yourself to the fullest within your individual

limits: that's the essence of running, and a metaphor for life — and for me, for writing as well. (83)

More frequently, I find examples that compare writing to running or running to writing, but rarely do I find an example where a third activity or concept is introduced. In this last case, Murakami is finding common ground for writing, running, and life as overlapping endeavors. Through one we can understand the other. In Murakami's side-by-side-by-side comparisons of these three, we see knowledge structuring. If you have extensive practice in one, such as running, you may be better positioned to understand writing by way of the parallels these activities share. Likewise, we might think of the challenges and victories we face as writers as a metaphor for the hardships and joys we experience in life, and vice versa when life becomes a metaphor for our running.

George Sheehan

Sheehan is a less well-known but no less illustrious example of a published author who wrote passionately about the relationship between physical activity and writing activity. Unlike Oates and Murakami, Sheehan is not a fiction writer. Although he is the author of several books and columns, Sheehan hardly takes his writing to the road when he needs to invent characters for plots and settings as the backdrop to conflicts for his readership because his work as a writer has existed in very different contexts—journalistic and medical ones, to be specific. Sheehan, who was running marathons and setting records well into his golden years, made his living primarily as a physician. His love of running, writing, and his medical expertise made him a desirable addition to the editorial staff of *Runner's World* magazine, and even when prostate cancer took away his ability to run in 1986, he wrote with a keen interest and intent to share his knowledge of running with public audiences. The title of his final book—*Going the Distance: One Man's Journey to the End of His Life*, published posthumously, exemplifies how a knowledge structure, one grounded in writing, can be used by a runner to convey information through writing. An earlier book of Sheehan's provides an illuminating description of how this prolific writer composed on the run:

Somehow, perhaps not the way I have said, running gives me the word, the phrase, the sentence that is just right. And there are times when I take a column on the road and it is like pulling the handle of a slot machine. Bang comes down the first sentence.

> Bang comes down the second, and the paragraphs unfold. And then Bang, jackpot, the piece is finished, whole and true and good." (3)

What some might consider a Herculean feat, trying to write a column while running, Sheehan considers a bonanza for his creative process. Again, he is creating a knowledge structure here by comparing running to another activity, in this case playing a slot machine, but within this knowledge structure we also witness how Sheehan operates as a generative thinker. What begins as a word becomes a phrase and then becomes a sentence before evolving into an entire column. Not all writers possess the ability to create an entire text while moving, and as Murakami stated, for some it is not about ability but preference. Sheehan may delight in thinking about his writing while running, but Murakami would rather not think about writing or anything at all. Still, both writers insist that running has helped their writing in mysterious and meaningful ways, but the words they use to describe this relationship vary considerably.

CONCLUSION

Throughout this chapter, I have delineated concepts, definitions, and analyzed examples to establish an embodied cognition framework that expands what we previously understood about the relationship between physical activity and writing activity. The illustrative published examples from Oates, Murakami, and Sheehan serve as a basis for understanding how all or part of the framework can be applied to professional writers hypothesizing about this relationship. In the next chapter, I will extend this analysis to include the experiences of other writers who have and have not had their minds fly with ideas for writing while on the run. The professional writers in the next chapter hail from several industries, including journalism, technical writing, children's literature, blogging, and academic writing.

5 Going Pro: Portraits of Successful Embodied Writers

At thirty-three weeks pregnant, I am wondering if I am as lost as I feel. I picture a soundbite on the news, "27-year-old pregnant woman eaten by bear in national forest."

On this curiously marked path in the Great Smoky Mountains, I pass one of a dozen fallen trees I've already seen, but just ahead of this one there's a sign.

> "Rapid motion through space elates one." — James Joyce

This corrugated plastic sign is one of many staked in the ground to confirm that I'm still on course. But when will I see the next one? These signs, posted by the 2017 Writers Who Run 10K Trail Race coordinators, sometimes relate loosely to the writing process or running. If I could, I'd take every one with me and plaster them to the walls of my office. Instead, I snap a few pictures.

Unlike Joyce, though, who has never had to bear the weight of another human between his pelvic bones or shift his spinal alignment forward enough to counterbalance an extra twenty pounds of blood, placenta, and amniotic fluid, I am neither elated nor rapid. The extra pounds I'm carrying are weighing me down. Sometimes I stop to walk up the steeper inclines, and when I do I lift my watermelon-sized bump up with both hands for some much needed pressure release. Maybe running a 6.2-mile race while mightily pregnant wasn't the smartest idea I've had.

And yet, all of the medical literature on exercise in pregnancy and my doctor's advice told me that it's okay to be trotting up the side of this never-ending gradient.[18] If I post anything to Facebook, I'm sure I'll incur the scrutiny of others. People think women's bodies shouldn't be running this far into a pregnancy, just as male colleagues of mine sneer at the thought of me writing my dissertation in this third trimester. How could I possibly have the energy reserves to run, write, and grow a child? They recommend I take some time off, but there is a point to be made. This is a hill I will not die on, but rather, will trot up successfully. This is the hill that challenges depictions of women's running bodies to be "white, thin, straight, fast, feminine, middle-class, and disciplined" (Faulkner 91). This hill is why my running and writing pregnant body makes people so uncomfortable.

I distract myself by thinking about my dissertation. Will I mention this run that took me through the mountains and the mists of an incoming hurricane? Will an audience of academics care about what my body went through? When my unborn son comes earthside, will I tell him one day he traveled with me through this muddy trek? Through my even messier dissertation?

These curiosities propel me forward.

INTRODUCTION

This chapter showcases four overlapping and contrasting, illustrative examples of professional writers who enact generative or restorative thinking while engaging in physical activity, and in many cases, these writers invoke a knowledge structure to convey meaning through shared embodied knowledge with participants. In each portrait, I offer a short introduction to each professional writer before sharing the most interesting and illustrative insights that materialized during our interviews. The first writer, *The Dallas Morning News* journalist Brentney Hamilton, was one who reported mostly generative thinking experiences while running, as opposed to the second writer, technical communication scholar Dr. Jordan Smith, who reported more restorative thinking experiences.[19] Next, I introduce a children's book author, Christie Wild, who examines what happens when a writer shifts more fluidly between generative thinking and restorative thinking. Wild, who is also a writing-running coach—frequently makes use of knowledge structures in her consultation work, which I will unpack in the final section featuring Dr. Thomas Gardner, a professor of literature at Virginia Tech University and a writer fascinated by the moments in writing and in running when people lose control of their body or their words.

Originally, my intention was not to interview primarily runners, but those who referred me to other potential study participants happened to know a writer in a running group who happened to know another runner-writer and so on. The referral process spiraled upwards and in the direction of running early on in my data collection process. It also struck me how much more excited my participants were to talk about writing in connection to running or walking. Other activities simply did not provide enough opportunity to let the mind wander, as *New York Magazine* writer Melissa Dahl conveyed and as will the first professional writer featured here.

Earlier, I also explained how Robert Boice's study of academic and non-academic writers informed my decision to study both types of writers. Although I identify as an academic writer now, about a decade ago I began my career as a features journalist for *The Kansas City Star*. I have seen the ways in which both academic and non-academic writers marvel at the power of sensorimotor movement to alter their writing processes in profound ways. For this reason, I tried to seek both academic and non-academic writers. Admittedly, finding more non-academic writers proved more challenging than finding academic ones, and my pool of professional writing participants leans in an academic direction. Like me, some of the writers I interviewed identify as both academic and non-academic writers. These identities are fluid, so I am hesitant to draw any conclusions about an academic or non-academic binary for writing studies, although it is worth acknowledging that some differences may exist.

PORTRAITS OF PROFESSIONAL WRITERS

Brentney Hamilton

Dallas Morning News journalist Brentney Hamilton is a key example of a professional writer who engages in primarily generative thinking practices while being physically active. Through a long, careful analysis of Hamilton's interview transcript, a few findings became clear: first, she is explicitly aware of the relationship between physical activity and writing activity. Second, she understands this relationship well enough to harness it for her own creative potential. Third, during physical activity she internally dissociates to engage in generative thinking about her writing.

I first met Hamilton at a *Dallas Morning News* get-together. The company was launching a vibrantly colored entertainment site that is still in operation, *Guidelive*, and we were talking over drinks about writing for our new, twenty-something target audience. Hamilton was more reserved than the other reporters I was meeting for the first time. She could not have been much taller than me—perhaps five feet three or four inches tall—with much longer, wavy light brown hair. Her general demeanor suggested that she was an old soul at heart, but one who was enjoying bursts of creative energy and industry as a young professional. After several years working as a full-time reporter and features editor, Hamilton discovered her strong preference for using physical activity as a form of generative thinking through marathon training. Hamilton had been a running company coach (while also working as a reporter) for several years, completing half marathons every few months and completing her first two full marathons with relative ease.

When I interviewed Hamilton, she had not been able to run for several weeks because she had entered her third trimester of pregnancy. Up until her twenty-third week, she continued to run, but since she recently stopped she had been using an elliptical machine to partially retain a level of physical fitness she found comfortable prior to her pregnancy. Still, she expressed both discontent with the elliptical and longed to return to running after giving birth to her child. She maintained a regular exercise program each week despite having a busier work schedule, a longer commute, and more physical constraints than she had ever experienced before. She fondly recalled the time when she was a freelance writer and able to take breaks from work to run, saying, "When I was a freelance writer for *Pegasus News*, I was contracted for twenty-nine hours a week, so I could go for a run whenever I wanted pretty much . . . that was like the peak of my productivity as a writer." At her new place of work, a gym was available in the office building, but she said she did not prefer using the gym as a workout space as much as she preferred running outside.[20]

For Hamilton, generative thinking occurs while running and thinking directly about her writing—even at various stages in the writing process. During our interview, Hamilton joked that she struggled to find motivation for any physical activity other than running. She quickly followed up with a slight modification to that answer, saying that she felt her imagination was challenged more by longer, endurance runs than by daily training runs. She explained:

> It's usually on a super long run which is part of a running program if you're training for a distance you haven't done before. So there have been plenty of times when, especially if you're running with a group, you can get into a trance and fall behind someone and then your mind wanders completely, and I've found sometimes that I've written entire chapters of things,

written and edited and sometimes been able to commit it to
memory because I thought about it so much.

Note that Hamilton is identifying her ability to engage in different
stages of the writing process while running, which includes the ability
to brainstorm ideas for writing, to draft writing, and then to edit her
writing in her head. While running, Hamilton is able to control various
cognitive experiences that support her writing process.

Hamilton, like several other professional writers in this study, said
she did not require a complex scientific understanding of the cognitive
science or neuroscience implicated in the relationship between writing
activity and physical activity in order to benefit from this relationship.
When asked to share her thoughts on the relationship between writing
activity and physical activity, Hamilton said, "It's not a conversation that
I really feel like I'm able to intellectually discuss because I don't understand the science well enough." The science, as discussed in Chapters
Two and Three, is too complex to pin on one brain structure or state
of mind, but we can think back to Brown's elaboration on internal and
external states of association and dissociation. When a writer, like Hamilton, "zones out" and begins to think about writing while running, she
is prepared to enter into a state of generative thinking. A term Hamilton
uses is "trance." There are numerous potential meanings tied to the word
trance, but, for our purposes, we might think of Hamilton's description
of a trance as a state of cognition in which she as a writer is becoming
more closely attuned to her writing. As a result, generative thinking can
occur because Hamilton enters into this state of internal dissociation
through the act of running, and it enables her to think about her writing.

Dr. Jordan Smith

So many of the writers who want to talk with me about the connections
they see between writing and running are creative writers—novelists,
poets, and features journalists, to list only a few. In Fall 2019, I reached
out to a few running friends in the field of technical communication
research to see if they knew of anyone who would be interested in being
interviewed about their writing and running practices, and that is how
I came to know Dr. Jordan Smith, a runner who had already hammered
out an interesting knowledge structure prior to our first face-to-face conversation, but whose restorative thinking potential stands in crisp contrast to the generative thinking propensities of Hamilton.

Smith is currently an Assistant Professor of Technical Communication at the University of North Texas, where he specializes in corpus linguistics, register variation, English grammar and usage, and technical editing. He introduced himself to me in an email, saying that he was interested in being a participant in my study, and the following spring we set up a time for our interview. Because we both currently reside in Denton, Texas, Smith was able to walk approximately two miles from his home in North Denton to my first-floor office on Texas Woman's University's campus. With a wide smile and a clean-shaven head, he offered me a handshake before taking a seat directly across from me at my conference table before we spent some time talking about his recent move to Denton, our shared alma mater (Iowa State University's Rhetoric and Professional Communication Graduate Program), and our lives as working academic parents before heading into our question-and-answer session.

To bring into fuller view the exercising and writing preferences of the writers I interviewed, the first two questions ask the participant to describe the typical physical activities they engage in during the week and on weekends.[21] At the time of our interview, Smith was still running each week, but he had taken a new interest in weightlifting during the workweek due in part to his interest in a smartphone app that teaches the technical elements and dynamic movements needed to master key weightlifting positions at the gym. On Saturdays, he carved out time for a longer run of six miles or so, a distance, he says, he used to consider an easy run compared to the thirty-mile runs he scheduled for himself in Iowa while he was training for his next marathon or ultramarathon.

After enough hours spent racking up his training miles and one terribly painful recovery that followed his first and last foray into the Ogden Full Marathon scene (a mostly downhill sloping course into the Ogden Canyon that caused extreme soreness in his knees), Smith asked himself if the marathon was the right distance for him. Prior to our meeting, he had developed his own knowledge structure to help himself make up his mind about the distance of half marathons and marathons by comparing these distances to different programs of graduate study. In the following example, he provides a knowledge structure for us to understand what he means:

> I think [the half marathon] is a nice distance. [For] me, I likened it to if a marathon is a PhD, a half marathon is a master's degree. I just think the master's degree is the perfect degree. It's

fun, you're engaged, you're doing this cool stuff but there isn't as much pressure as there was in the PhD. . . . It was fun when I finished, and I felt really good about myself for the master's and the half marathon. And with the PhD, parts of it were just a real slog, so I'd like to do half marathons again.

Similar to the other knowledge structures dissected in the previous chapter, Smith's knowledge structure in this example compares two ostensibly separate activities—running long distances and spending several years of one's life in an intensive program of graduate writing—and makes a meaningful comparison between the two to better describe to his listener what he means. Going the distance in a master's program feels fun and engaging to Smith, who likely trained very well for that distance to finish it with relative ease and enjoyment. The master's degree, he says, was also enough time spent engaging in intellectual inquiry to be stimulating without feeling like the "real slog" that the PhD became. To Smith, these running distances and graduate programs of study resemble one another. With me as his audience—someone who has finished a master's and a doctoral degree, and who has run a half marathon, but not a marathon—he likely inferred that I can relate to some of these experiences we share. What I cannot relate to, the feeling of having run a full marathon, I can begin to understand through this knowledge structure he shares, and thus, I can use my past sensorimotor experiences to connect with what he describes.

Despite this insightful knowledge structure Smith has developed, generative thinking was not a mode of thinking that he fell into naturally as a runner-writer. In our interview, he pondered the synergistic potential of his running and writing activity, but he said he had not observed himself thinking about writing much while he ran:

> Most of the time I'm listening to music or a podcast, and I'm not just letting my mind go. I don't know that I'm a really I-gotta-go-for-a-run-to-clear-my-head-type of person. I will say, though, for me a run—if I'm contrasting a run with a gym workout—a run does feel more conducive to head clearing and having ideas or inspiration strike. . . . I don't know how my physical activity and my writing activity are related other than I believe that if I'm physically active, then I'm healthier and should be able to focus better. And I think that would help me be a better writer.

Personal experience tells me that it is infinitely harder for me to develop my raw ideas for writing while listening to podcasts than it is to have a familiar song or instrumental music echoing around between my ears. Over a decade of teaching writing at the college level also confirms that most students struggle to focus on an in-class writing assignment if the background music contains lyrics—or if there is any background music or noise at all, for that matter. It can be challenging to pin down our own words as we consume the words of others. What Smith casually mentions at the end of this statement, though, interests me.

Much like Hamilton, Smith doesn't purport to understand the relationship between physical activity and writing activity, but he believes that the former benefits from the latter. Despite comparing the two activities in the previously discussed knowledge structure, Smith goes on to describe these activities as distinctly different from one another but similar in their ability to invoke restorative thinking:

> Writing for me is very much an office-type desk job thing. When I'm writing, I'm not the type that takes off with his laptop places. I'm just at a desk in my office writing. So that's the writing part. It's sedentary for me. The physical activity really helps to turn on my brain in some ways. I know that the physical activity is good for me to be healthy so I can stay focused.

For Smith, time spent running or even lifting weights is like a preventative measure taken to ensure his overall writing health. He prefers for the two activities to not bleed into each other, but he is confident that the time he spends exercising, and therefore deliberately not thinking about his writing, allows him to return to a draft in a focused way. Physical activity turns on his brain, he claims, which is a necessary step to be taken before he writes. For this reason, Smith falls in line with the description of a restorative thinker.

Toward the end of our interview, Smith told me that if there was one type of physical activity he could see himself employing as a way to think about his writing that activity would have to be walking. Walking, as discussed in Chapter Four, may be more conducive to generative and restorative thinking for some writers because the activity is more accessible to more bodies than running is, running being more demanding of one's focus and attention to rapid movement through space, patterns of pacing, and breathwork. This parting thought emphasizes, to me, however, that the opportunity to generate new ideas for one's writing while walking, running, or engaging in any other form of physical activity is often an overlooked possibility. In education, we do not train writers to identify these moments of embodied cognition potential. In the industries of writing and publishing, little dialogue on embodied writing exists. Perhaps this missed opportunity is due to the overwhelming number of lessons to be shared about sustainable writing practices. With countless approaches to or best practices on invention, development, style, organization, delivery, genre, and more, we hardly have time to ponder how the body feels while writing in sedentary positions or physical dynamic movements. This glaring gap in the development of any writer is too often overlooked.

Worth noting is that the styles and genres of writing typically performed by our first two writers, Hamilton and Smith, are markedly distinct. As a features journalist, Hamilton writes about arts and entertainment topics, covering local events at music venues, museums, and restaurants. As a technical communicator and scholar, Smith takes a page from a different book, one that is more explicit and avoids implied meaning. To wit, Hamilton can be running and thinking of creative titles or conclusions derived from a pun that makes the topic of her coverage more humorous and more lighthearted than before she took the run, whereas Smith can't take such a risk, which might mislead his audience. Perhaps the specificity and detail of technical writing and editing doesn't lend well to the act of creating or revising such writing while in motion. The possibility can't be ruled out entirely, of course, but we might think about how generative and restorative thinking presented in these first two portraits might be controlled by various styles and genres of writing.

Christie Wright Wild

As a children's picture book writer, novelist, and avid blogger, Wild presents yet another differing account of writing-and-running experiences, especially since shifting between generative and restorative thinking can occur more fluidly than we might be led to understand by Hamilton's and Smith's portraits alone. Wild's portrait is also useful to our understanding of running and walking for writing because her experiences give glimpses into how knowledge structuring equips the professional writer with a useful embodied cognition strategy for understanding writerly growth.

Wild, through her narrowly rounded eyeglasses and her medium-length waves of soft brown hair, has a contagious laugh that echoes through the halls of Fontana Village Resort in North Carolina, where her Annual Writers Who Run Retreat takes place in June. Wild founded the retreat in hopes that she could help other writers reimagine a long day's worth of writing. In particular, she asks retreat participants to meet at the front of the resort each morning for a two-mile run or walk. The one summer I served as a faculty member at this retreat, I vividly remember having conversations about writing with other writers on these cool, dewy runs through short paths of the Appalachian Trail. We discussed the projects and goals that lay ahead of us and the faculty workshops that punctuated their writing sessions.

While the retreat is underway, Wild spends a great deal of time talking with writers about their practices as writers and runners or walkers to figure out how she can better support this unique demographic. Throughout the year and leading up to the retreat, she hosts a "Writers Who Run RETREAT" Facebook group to connect writers from all over the country by posting writing- or running-themed content and encouraging others to post about the positive effects of physical activity on the brain and questions relevant to writing or running habits. At times she posts a "Daily Mile Marker Check-in," asking the group members to be accountable to their practices by sharing progress in either writing or running with this unique community. Wild has even facilitated numerous instructional webinars for this community to share scientific research and personal testimony in support of writers who find physical exercise to be their preferred creative outlet. Because our interest in the relationship between physical activity and writing activity aligns so closely, I approached her with an invitation to interview with me for this project. In our conversation, I found that we were both searching for a theoretical framework to explain the highly variable, shapeshifting nature of this relationship, a theory and terminology that would help us convey what we had individually internalized as a kind of embodied knowledge we thought a larger community of runner-writers could relate to.

What was most remarkable about my conversations with Wild was her ability to shift between generative thinking and restorative thinking with ease and fluidity. In one example of shifting that Wild shared with me, she recalled the story of a runner who was struggling with boredom while running outside on trails, an admission she found shocking.[22] Wild said she could not fathom that someone could be bored outdoors, and she described, in her own words, generative thinking and restorative thinking:

> Somebody was asking the question of "What do you do when
> . . . [you] get so bored during runs—even hav[ing] music and
> all this stuff with nature? And I'm like: Uhhhh, really? How
> do you get bored? Maybe I'm crazy or something but I'm al-
> ways thinking about something. Either templates or distance
> and miles and trying to do the math and all that kind of stuff.
> Or I'm working on a story or a personal problem, you know, I'm
> always trying to work something out in my mind. And if I'm
> not, I'm enjoying the nature, like: Oh, a flower! Oh, this . . . Oh,
> that. . . . It's the smallest things that can cheer me up or make
> me happy. . . . How can I get bored?

Undoubtedly, Wild possesses strong convictions about her internal thought processes while she runs. With a hint of sarcasm, Wild begins bewildered, marveling at the idea of not having enough pre-existing knowledge to fill one's mind or no desire to perform cognitive tasks while running. She quickly alludes to her writing when she mentions the blogging templates she works with (for freelance blogging and ghostwriting work), and then we can see how her thoughts sway in another direction, such as how she is processing her running progress. She describes how her brain can then jump to a story idea that she is working on, or at least entertaining as a potential story worth writing, before darting away from the writing to a personal problem.

Wild's shifts between generative and restorative thinking is demonstrative of several new ideas related to embodied cognition. First, one can imagine that this knowledge-making process is generative in that she is coming to know or create her writing while moving through a rapidly changing sensorimotor experience. She notices the nature around her and lets her attention stray from generating new ideas until she is ready to return to the act of generative thinking for her writing once again. Her personal problems are also somewhat generative because she is creating thoughts and ideas to improve those problems, but we cannot say that this kind of generative thinking creates new ideas for her writing process—only that it restores her emotional brain for improved cognitive focus on her writing later.

Second, Wild also suggests she engages in restorative thinking in this description, too, giving us reason to believe that her generative and restorative thinking tendencies slide along a continuum. In describing restorative thinking as a kind of cognitive off-loading, she mentions thinking about a phase of her writing process that she needs to divert her cognitive capacity away from, redirecting her cognitive focus on running in terms of distance and mileage, and only returning to writing again when she has off-loaded attention long enough to return with a fresh mind to her writing task. Wild's discussion of generative-restorative shifting suggests that a spectrum of embodied cognition exists. Wild was one of several participants who discussed, in her own words, using knowledge structuring and cognitive off-loading strategies within a single physical activity session. Recall that in Chapter Four I discussed how these two strategies lead to generative and restorative thinking, respectively, so we can think of these strategies as the vessels—or to use a running term, the relay batons—with which we give our minds permission to pass into a generative or a restorative state of thinking as we move away from or past the work we have left behind on our pages. Therefore, it would behoove us to imagine a spectrum of generative-restorative activity in which some embodied writers find themselves consciously and unconsciously shifting between generative and restorative effects, whereas other writers report spending more time on either the generative or restorative end of this activity spectrum. This means that other writers consistently spend more time involved in generative thinking or restorative thinking while exercising.[23]

We must discuss generative-restorative shifting if we want to paint a more accurate depiction of the embodied writing processes of writers as diversified as the bodies from which they write. There is no singular or correct way to run and write, to walk and write, or to lie perfectly still and write. All bodies come bearing different levels of sensorimotor ability or disability. When we tap into embodied ways of thinking —generative, restorative, or moving more fluidly between both—we are able to contemplate what our writing bodies need. Wild's thoughts about writing or her natural surroundings while running reveal more about how generative and restorative shifting work, at times giving us reason to question how other professional writers shift between generative and restorative thinking as an extension of their writing processes. We should notice, too, that her generative-restorative shifting occurs for a writing project already in progress; this exigency suggests that the effects of physical activity on the writing process are not limited to prewriting creative development, post-writing revision, or any other stage of the writing process. Rather, generative-restorative shifting comes into play at various stages of her writing process. Because she coaches other writers, she gives us reason to believe that she is not an anomaly, but rather, that other writers experience such shifting at various stages of the writing process, too.

In terms of timing—morning, afternoon, or evening preferences for exercise times—Wild contends that it matters little when writers can engage in physical activity. What matters more is how the writer takes control of their thoughts while engaged in generative thinking or how the writer relinquishes control over their mind when restorative thinking is preferred. Just as writers embrace different writing processes, the writers Wild coaches through her retreat all utilize physical activity differently, at different times, and based on different personal preferences, and implicit to this claim is that differences between writing processes matter minimally so long as the writers feel as though they are benefiting from regular running and writing practices. Shortly after Wild's narration of her own writing process as generative-restorative shifting—in which she claimed that she can easily switch between generative and restorative thinking about her writing process while running—she expanded her reasoning from her particular experience to the more generalized experiences of other writers she has coached at her retreat. She explained:

> Some people will run first thing in the morning, just to get it out of the way, and then their writing session[s] [are] better. And then some people do their writing, and then they go for a run, and then they can work out the problems that they stopped at in the writing . . . Their brains are continually writing as they go on a run. I guess as you do it on a daily basis, [the running] kind of gets [you] into a cycle and each element feeds into each element, and [the elements] continue to help each other out.

Exercising prior to embarking on the day's writing journey could be considered both a generative and a restorative way of thinking, opening the door for generative-restorative shifting, but not necessarily to occur simultaneously. If engaging in generative thinking, the pre-writing exerciser can consciously create content for writing in the session to come. Conversely, Wild gives the contrary example of the restorative thinker who could be subconsciously off-loading the weight of an intellectually draining writing task to make the return to writing as easy as possible. In the second scenario, cognition occurs and continues as a function of the writing through generative thinking on the part of the write-early, run-later exercisers. So again, we are seeing that generative-restorative shifting does not necessarily occur simultaneously and that sometimes one way of thinking can be preferred over the other. In Wild's second scenario, the clear preference is for restorative thinking over generative thinking. More interestingly, Wild recognizes the potential benefits in both approaches to this sort of embodied cognition, and in her role as a writing coach she supports the idea that different writers need different ways of connecting their writing processes to their physical activity sessions, especially in terms of timing. Therefore, the greatest lesson to be learned from this example is that physical activity benefits writing activity, no matter the time of day.

Much like Smith, Wild embraced knowledge structuring as a way to make explicit and comprehensible the embodied knowledge of writing and running that she wanted to share with others. In November, 2016, I joined one of Wild's virtual coaching webinars, titled "3 Simple Secrets Successful Authors Know That Help Them Avoid Procrastination, Frustration, and Rejection."[24] Throughout her webinar, I noted how Wild shared numerous examples of knowledge structuring and did so very consciously and intentionally.[25] One slide in particular struck me as rife with knowledge structures and provided me with ideas for using knowledge structuring in my embodied writing classroom. This slide begins with a picture of smiling, bouncy runners as the focal point of the left-side of the screen and a subheading that read: "Take Runners for Example," before making the following points:

- They train.
- Hills, tempo, speedwork, drills, long runs.
- "Active Rest" vs. "Creative Baby."

The "They" referred to on this slide points to runners in general. What is listed in the second bullet are types of running training exercises that are more sophisticated than simply running on a flat trail. Hills build stronger leg and gluteal muscles needed to improve for other intervals, such as timed speedwork drills. A tempo run tracks along at a pace that is twenty-five to thirty seconds slower than a runner's best time per mile and is used to determine a reliable pace for a runner to take when running for an hour or more. These first two bullets aid in Wild's knowledge structuring; she helps writers understand and improve their writing processes by understanding how marathoners, like herself, train for long-distance races. Her comparison of writing to running synthesizes the two activities in relatable terms, and ultimately we gain from Wild's knowledge structuring the ability to see how physical activity informs and even structures writing activity, highlighting to those who are unaware of this relationship the latent value of knowledge structuring as a strategy for extracting meaning from physical activity.

Wild also draws from the words of writers to further substantiate her use of knowledge structuring. Perhaps the clearest example of knowledge structuring via other writers' experiences occurs when she cites Caldecott Award-winning children's book author Jane Yolen, who says, "Exercise the writing muscle every day, even if it is only a letter, notes, a title list, a character sketch, a journal entry. Writers are like dancers, like athletes. Without that exercise, the muscles seize up." Yolen's suggestion that the writer is like the dancer or the athlete underscores her insinuation that there is a metaphorical muscle all writers have that must be trained every day; otherwise, that muscle weakens and loses capability over time. The logic within this metaphor can be broken down as follows: writers are similar to dancers and athletes; exercise your brain every day in the same way a dancer or athlete would exercise their essential muscle groups; eventually the writer becomes stronger for exercising their writing muscle in the same way dancers and athletes do by exercising their physical muscles. Those three logical premises build on one another like steps, structuring a short, accessible staircase by which any writer can take one step at a time.

Wild's third bullet point ("Active Rest" vs. "Creative Baby") provides a knowledge structure for understanding restorative thinking in writers and runners. The concepts are presented side-by-side because they are related, but one will be more easily recognizable to runners than the other. Colloquially, active rest is a term used by runners to explain how to exercise on days when a training run is not scheduled. Some runners swim, others cycle, and some go for easy strolls through their neighborhood. The idea of active rest is to let the larger muscles that have been overtaxed by running be repaired but not to let the body go completely without any exercise or movement because light movement stimulates repair and growth of new cells by ensuring the transport of blood, glycogen, and restorative nutrients, such as potassium, to the damaged muscles. Lack of movement decreases the motility of blood, glycogen, and necessary nutrients. If a runner takes every Sunday off from a daily running routine, they then use that time to effectively recover from and heal any damage sustained to the muscle tissue with gentle walking activity, or massage, or in some cases exercising underutilized muscle groups, such as arm or back muscles. In a similar manner, writers must make use of active rest, too. Writers will understand the concept of creative baby to mean an idea for a larger writing project that must be nurtured with consistent attention and deeper thinking at various points throughout one's day because forgetting to care for these ideas leads to atrophy. The nurturing of a creative baby happens when we take time off from a more demanding writing project we have been working on, which in turn gives our mind (the writing muscle) time to rest by letting it dwell on a new idea. Again, there is knowledge structuring in the third bullet that clearly compares active rest, in running, to creative babies, in writing, from which a writer or runner can understand writing or running practices in terms of running and writing, respectively.

Dr. Thomas Gardner

Of all the writers participating in my study, Dr. Gardner is the most aware of the relationship between writing and physical activity, especially in terms of how generative thinking can be achieved through cognitive control. Gardner is an endurance runner, an alumnus of and a distinguished professor at Virginia Tech University, and the author of several books on poetry—including a book of lyrical essays that received some acclaim in *The Atlantic* article I referenced in Chapter One. After reading his book of essays on running, titled *Poverty Creek Journal*, which features fifty-two essays or one essay for every week of the year he spent journaling about poetic and personal thoughts entertained while he was running, I sent him a formal email request to participate in this project. I was heartened to learn of his willingness to participate and to learn that he, too, has wondered for years about the effects of physical activity on the writer's process.

Although I never had the opportunity to meet Gardner in person, the picture of him on the back of his book displays a very tall, almost lanky man who remains in strong physical condition even as he approaches retirement. His brown hair is kept short, and he wears eyeglasses when needed. Not one to misuse or waste words, Gardner was laconic at first, but our discussion provoked more words, warmth, and friendliness as our conversation deepened.

In his writing, Gardner exhibits a well-integrated, non-dualistic appreciation of the role of the body in the mind's work of writing, which is carried through in his writing in *Poverty Creek Journal*. During our interview, Gardner told me that his thinking on the relationship between running and writing did influence his essays for the book and that he wrote about this relationship in the online reader's companion to his book provided by his publisher. In this companion, he relives a moment in his young adulthood when an English professor complimented him on his results in the Penn Relays, the oldest and largest collegiate track and field competition in the United States (so well known, in fact, that his race results were published in *The New York Times*). Gardner remembers feeling a little embarrassed, but he also thinks of that moment as a turning point when he stopped "walling off the various parts of [his] life," deciding to permit himself "to move back and forth between body and spirit, body and mind, using one to metaphorically unfold and speak back to the other, and vice versa" (3). He credits his peaceful acceptance of each of these parts of himself as a support mechanism for his writing, his teaching of literature, and his musings in *Poverty Creek Journal*.

In several ways, what Gardner has expressed here relates to Robert Yagelski's discussion of the mind-body disconnect in *Writing as a Way of Being*. Yagelski, who in his book saw the advent of standardized testing as the primary culprit of disembodied writing, argues that our first encounters with writing should occur in the wilds of our own imaginations. Too often instead, we discover how to write at desks functioning as disembodied casts of our own making. A more holistic writing process would integrate the body and mind through the movement of embodied cognition. Likewise, Gardner confirms that reuniting mind and body in the writing process makes for a well-integrated, non-dualistic appreciation of the role of the body in the mind's work of writing. Recall that, according to Bazerman and Tinberg, embodied cognition "assumes complex mental processes at work, then embodied cognition draws in addition upon the physical and affective aspects of the composing process" (74). Gardner believes that his running generates the shape of his poetry. He notices how "a poem . . . gives us instructions for reenacting its inner movements," saying that "we 'do' the poem in our own minds and bodies, gradually coming to understand, for ourselves, how its parts fit together as a coherent action" (Gardner 7). His statements in this journal have a physicality all their own, taking shape, almost rolling off the page just as we could imagine them rolling off the tongue when we say them out loud. Gardner said he takes special care to ensure that his words in this statement reflect the physical movement he feels as he crafts them, or the movement he hopes to stir in his reader, by crafting syntactical structures that reflect metrical, almost musical repetitions of sound. Gardner taps into generative ways of thinking derived from decades spent running to achieve the effects of generative thinking that allow him to craft his writing in this uncommon but provocatively embodied way.

Seasoned runner-writers have come forward to verify Gardner's writing about running as a generative way of thinking and to speak to the power of his embodied claims. He said he found the greatest sense of validation when a reviewer for *The New Yorker* dubbed his book, "One of the better books about running I've read, and the only one to uncover the literary possibilities inside the terse, repetitive, normally unimaginative genre of the running log" (Schulz). Reading this quotation, Gardner said he was elated to see another writer relating to "the way [his] mind moves when [he] run[s]," meaning that he appreciated most connecting with another writer who uses running as a way of harnessing generative thinking. And yet, despite all the acclaim he received, he was hesitant to draw firm conclusions about embodied cognition in relation to his writing process, but he did affirm that running helps him write. He preferred to explore the relationship between writing activity and physical activity more poetically and daily, every morning when he laces up his sneakers. In this way, Gardner's writing models new ways to enact embodied cognition during the creation process, and we see this reflected in the way he crafts his words, clauses, sentences, and paragraphs. This ability to compose in such an embodied way may come more easily to Gardner because he has taken pause to reflect on the connections that exist between running and writing, and he has externalized those connections with the written word. Over several decades of active thinking, writing, and sharing his embodied writing with others, he has amassed a storehouse full of generative thinking strategies that not only strengthen his writing practice but have served up bountiful fodder for his writing.

Generative Thinking and Control. To add to his idea that poetry imitates running, Gardner briefly alludes to the idea that running brings a writer closer to understanding writing because both endeavors require the practitioner to surrender control. Toward the end of his book of essays, he gives us one of the more concrete examples of what surrendering control feels like:

47: November 17, 2012

> The Roanoke half marathon. I've been pointing toward this race all fall but ended up running in a fair amount of pain and slower than I'd hoped—1:49, about 8:20 per mile. At some point, in almost every race, you get lost. You open your eyes and realize you're in trouble. Your heart rate rises, your concentration buckles, and you're suddenly flailing around inside, with no landmark save for a familiar hatred of yourself and the ego that made you line up and race. . . . The body does have limits, and your fingers will eventually fumble everything you love. But go on and think of what you could build there, "sentence by shunning sentence," your words most alive where they're most disappointed in themselves. Why else would you race? Why go back there, year after year?

The quotation "sentence by shunning sentence" is taken from American philosopher Stanley Cavell, who famously claimed that Emerson was the philosopher of the sentence, and that Emerson's philosophy circled around the idea of building worlds through sentences (134). Gardner is describing his own world building, too, albeit through the act of running. Running, like writing, is a dance of control to Gardner. When he loses control, he comments that his words are "disappointed in themselves," in the same way his "fingers will eventually fumble,"—a more sensorimotor description—and his runner's body will discover its limits at some point in every race. He draws these comparisons to make a larger point, which is this: running and writing challenge his sense of control for the improvement of his writing. For instance, he has built a world for himself as a runner, and that world has translated into his writing in his book of essays. As a result, he has been challenged and made to be vulnerable both as a runner and a writer. What has come of this vulnerability is a curiosity about what challenges his sense of control in running and writing. He enjoys surrendering his control enough to repeat doing so. As a runner, he seems to build a world for himself, one in which he understands his lack of control to be exhilarating or stressful, at times, but also filled with teachable moments. With this entry, he claims that running and writing are similar activities, and the way he begins with a running lesson that evolves into a writing lesson shows how he sometimes uses running experiences to reason, rationalize, or otherwise draw close logical comparisons between his running and his writing. In essence, running brings him nearer to understanding writing through close comparison.

Gardner's ability to think about writing while he runs and to write his thoughts down after he runs designates him as a primarily generative thinker. I gathered this much while rereading one of the few conclusions he was willing to offer during our interview, which happened to be a knowledge structure that compares running to poetry. Gardner began by explaining his emotions when a run goes badly. Imagine any reason a run could go badly for a runner, such as poor weather conditions, overly ambitious mileage projections, or "hitting the wall" in a longer race, negative self-talk, or brooding thoughts: these most negative conditions or thoughts are the ones Dr. Gardner said he likes to pay attention to when he runs. He said,

> I think about that a lot and the reason why is because poetry, which is what I teach, is all about that sort of thing, too. Frost makes a living by going into places where he's not in control, and sort of staying there for a while and then coming out alive and a lot different. Writers are interested in those same places, you know? They do it with words and emotions, and I do, too, but it turns out that you also do it with your body. Sometimes your body gives you ways of thinking about it in ways that your words and emotions don't.

Gardner's knowledge structuring in this statement makes for a strong comparison to states of being that challenge one's sense of control, particularly when he calls on the great works of Robert Frost to certify his opinion. Gardner's interest in situations that divest us of our control over our poetry, running, or life are those situations that motivate him to compose poems and to teach poetry as well as to run and to generate new ideas related to his running. He gains new insights by grappling with these difficulties, which he finds intellectually and creatively stimulating. When he says that "it turns out you also do it with your body," he is referring to his surprise in finding embodied cognition strategies within himself to use in his writing. He also mentioned that he spent the first ten years of his career trying to figure out how his "mind worked," as in not sitting at a desk waiting for ideas to come. Once he figured out that movement supported his writing, Gardner said, "Things have just kind of come flowing out of me."

Everyday Movement and Generative Thinking. Although this chapter focuses on many insights from long-distance runners, I end this last portrait by emphasizing that generative thinking is not limited to exceptionally gifted athletic or otherwise able-bodied individuals. As a matter of fact, many of the participants in this study reported experiencing embodied cognition while engaging in less physically intense movement patterns. Gardner mentioned that ideas that come to him as he is walking sometimes. New insights for his writing often strike after a hard day of writing in his office, when he walks outside to his car to go home. He said,

> The other thing that I've discovered and has happened over and over for years is that when I spend a day writing, and it often doesn't go well, when I walk the five or ten minutes to my car I often find that using my body will spring an idea that I wasn't able to get at my desk. So, there'll be days [when I'm] walking to my car and I have to pull out a pad and write something down. And I look like a true eccentric . . . I really do. I was out walking one day, eating an apple, and the idea I'd been struggling with for the past two hours came to me, and my department chair came by and there I am. You know, saliva dripping from the apple, looking like a madman, and she just kind of raised her eyebrow and kept on walking.

In this quick aside, Gardner vividly recounts one of the more memorable times when the act of generative thinking caused him to physically stop and write. In the beginning of his account, he mentions that this is a frequent occurrence for him, noting so with a tone of surprise at the time. He explains that these generative moments tend to happen when his ability to generate ideas for writing could not be forced to come forward while sitting at his desk. He laughs at himself, but his tone of voice is rather serious in underscoring how eccentric he must look, giving us pause to wonder: Why is moving to think thought to be eccentric in the first place? Whatever the reason may be, this instance of generative thinking was shared with me to demonstrate that Gardner experiences embodied cognition not just on a run while he is consciously aware of his movement and processing his writing. Instead, he highlights the ways in which embodied cognition surprises him time and again, meaning that this example is one of probably several times in Dr. Gardner's professional life when he stopped and appreciated the degree to which embodied cognition can happen without intentionally trying to control or to make it happen. When he feels stuck and can no longer think about his writing, he moves away from his desk only to generate new knowledge spontaneously. Generative thinking, then, need not always be planned. In the case of Gardner, we see how a professional writer has the ability to tap into conscious awareness of the relationship between writing and physical activity. Likewise, we see how a professional writer who is used to maintaining control over his writing process can experience embodied cognition spontaneously, just when he lets go of his ability to control his writing process.

CONCLUSION

With generative thinking, conscious reflection on one's embodied ways of moving and writing is of paramount importance when harnessing the latent potential of the relationship between physical activity and writing activity. Gardner is a successful example of how writers come to learn embodied methods of writing with or without theoretical terminology to define their experiences. Throughout this chapter, we have taken a critical look at the embodied cognition strategies used by professional writers, those who employ these strategies in a variety of ways and apply them to varying writing contexts and purposes. The data from these interviews does not just confirm existing scholarship on embodied writing and creativity processes but expands our understanding of how our physical activity patterns come to bear on our writing outcomes, particularly through shifts between generative and restorative thinking, using and applying knowledge structures, and taking conscious control over these embodied cognition strategies to approach our embodied writing processes with more intentionality.

The next chapter brings a shift in the generative-restorative thinking preferences of student writers. Restorative thinking will amble out onto the main stage to showcase what is possible when a student writer taps into embodied cognition strategies that support generative thinking. As seen in the examples of professional writers teaching writing, the momentum behind embodied writing is barreling forward and student interest in embodied writing pedagogy is soon to follow.

6 Learning Hurdles: Novice Writers Practicing Embodied Writing

From my upstairs bedroom, I can hear the storm door ricochet off the front door frame with a loud, wiry clap. Rebecca, my red-headed college roommate of three years, dropped her Nikes on the one-hundred-year-old wood floors of our downstairs living room before flinging herself onto our jet black futon to catch her breath, for just a moment prior to yelling upstairs to me about how miserably humid it is outside. Almost every afternoon for the last week she'd jetted off on these short runs, sundering her days in class from her evenings spent studying with these healthful excursions.

I sat as still as a sloth on a limb, tired and slightly hunched over my laptop. I'd been staring at the screen to work on my senior honors thesis for the last five hours, cozied up to a row of musty library books stacked haphazardly on top of mismatched binders. Nothing sounded less appealing than a springtime jog through our Brookside neighborhood of Kansas City, Missouri. But having been tethered to my writing post for far too long with too little to show for it, I also didn't feel like writing anymore. My body and mind had grown sore from sitting still trying to put words onto the page. I thought, "Can a run hurt any more than my lower body feels?"

Thirty minutes later, I was beading with sweat. My lungs were crisping at their edges from increased heat exposure. My shins were moving about as well as bags of dry concrete dust, but a combination of pride and curiosity willed me forward another block, and then another. I was wondering if everyone hurt this bad when they ran. I was wondering when I could expect a runner's high to take over. How much longer could I wait? Should I have just stayed home to write?

Lapping around a few city blocks felt painfully hard that first time around our neighborhood on foot, but the second time my lungs felt a little less fried and my legs felt a little less heavy. The third time I realized I could distract myself with new routes that took me by friends' apartments and city parks, and by my fourth run I became hooked on the feelings that came with running: the feeling of running away from a difficult problem or task, the cognitive release, the feeling of falling into a flow-like rhythm of movement with my thoughts, and sometimes, the feeling of running headlong into a difficult problem I needed to parse.

When I'm running, I visualize my writer's brain like a dog on a leash. Sometimes my brain tries to wander off course and think about relationships with friends or my grocery list, but when I notice this happening I remember to pull back on the leash, recentering my attention on the day's writing project. Why? Because just before I graduated from the University of Missouri—Kansas City, I learned something about writing that I never encountered in a textbook: I do my best thinking when I am on the move. At a desk—or on a couch, in a bed, or anywhere where I am seated or reclined—my mind tends to tire, to freeze, and to become more easily distracted by email. At a fast running pace, my distractions are fewer. Tiny bolts of creativity strike at least a few times on every run. I tune in regularly so I can catch those flashes of writerly insight.

I have also found focus as a writer on my yoga mat. Usually, when I am practicing yoga, I am not trying to think about my writing at all. In fact, I often find myself choosing to do yoga on mornings when I feel the most cognitively overwhelmed by writing projects. In a sun salutation series, my inhalations and exhalations help me move through forward bends and twisting poses with the intention of uniting body with breath. As a former yoga teacher, I trained practitioners to focus on the breath as a way of connecting with the body more and a way of inviting students to "zone out."[26] Of course, distracting thoughts will always return to our minds, but the goal of yoga poses and yogic control of the breath is to experience the present moment, not the writing that is to come. For me, this means not thinking about the writing I must do tomorrow or the draft I submitted yesterday. Instead, I do my best to ignore those writing-related distractions so that I can create space in my mind for new writing tasks after yoga ends.

INTRODUCTION

All writing is embodied and can benefit from the embodied cognition strategies presented in the last two chapters. Being a physically active writer at any age or of any ability level means a writer can connect their writing activity to their physical activity and do so in a way that supports their embodied cognition experiences as a writer. Writers who cannot make these connections may simply lack instruction and ongoing support. How can a tennis player learn proper forehand and backhand strokes if a coach has never introduced the technique and corrected form? In this chapter, I present four profiles of student writers who engaged in generative thinking, restorative thinking, or knowledge structures in transformative ways.[27] Through an analysis of my findings, I start to piece together what the relationship between physical activity and writing activity looks like for student writers of different abilities and backgrounds. As opposed to the generative thinking preferences of professional writers, the student writers I studied demonstrate strong preferences for restorative thinking. This preference neither rules out the possibility of generative thinking's potential nor the students' ability to create knowledge structures. In fact, I found traces of generative thinking and knowledge structuring in the written work of several students. By the end of this chapter, I hope to imbue readers with examples of embodied cognition as it unfolds in the writing processes of students. Writers or teachers of writing will be better positioned to enact embodied cognition if they see through these sundry examples that embodied cognition looks and feels a little different for every writer.

TEACHING EMBODIMENT

Student writers can connect their writing to their sensorimotor experiences in countless ways, ones as simple as standing to stretch when a writing task becomes too cognitively taxing or even handwriting a draft before typing the piece on a computer. In my classrooms, I have used yoga and meditation before writing activities to prepare student writers for the act of invention or brainstorming, and after writing activities I have led students in mindfulness-based games that require students to separate themselves physically from their writing before reflecting on what they have written. Almost every semester, I like to ask students to take a mindful walk, stroll, roll, or to engage in whatever form of forward motion or stillness is available to them, and I always ask them to try to think about their writing while moving if they are able. Many of these activities I adapted from colleagues in contemplative studies and religious studies departments, but there is limited scholarship on the pedagogical potential of these activities in writing classes.

An expanded perspective of embodied cognition is in order, one that might help writers and scholars understand embodied cognition as it pertains to the writing process. As a college composition professor and a former yoga teacher, I can confidently say that it is far easier for me to teach a mind than it is to teach a body. When I taught in my home yoga studio—Radiant Sun Academy, formerly known as Yogali—my focus was on my yoga students' physical alignment, the intentional sequencing of poses that built on other poses, cueing inhalations and exhalations, familiarizing myself with previous injuries or histories of bodily trauma that might impact their movement patterns, and preventing potential new injuries. Teaching yoga keeps my mind busy. Teaching writing also keeps my mind busy as I am thinking about nonverbal communication with students, scanning the room for students whose attention I need to regain, frequently returning to the student learning outcomes that guide our work, and simultaneously processing my own ideas on various aspects of the craft of writing (such as context, purpose, audience, style, organization and other rhetorical considerations) as I present those to my students. However, teaching writing in tandem with physical movement has revealed to me the challenges of introducing college students to embodied writing, but my experiences assure me that the challenges never eclipse the benefits felt by students.

At the forefront of this chapter, I want to point out that teaching embodied writing in college can be met with student resistance because there is no wide-sweeping call to promote embodied cognition in primary, secondary, or post-secondary education programs in the United States. Research confirms that embodied cognition-inspired pedagogies are the exception, not the standard, despite the calls for change being made on the part of psychologists and teacher advocates (McClelland et al., Mull and Smith). In *Teaching with Tenderness*, Becky Thompson has documented the "initial skepticism" students show when approached with the idea of moving their bodies in the classroom, stemming from our shared histories in educational settings where "a quiet, receptive mind is connected to a still and relaxed body" as opposed to seeing the classroom "as a living, breathing space" for movement and growth (59, 7). Before introducing any embodied writing assignment to students, I often wonder how many will approach embodied writing activities with a sense of curiosity and openness, and I wonder about how many will be confronted with feelings of internal resistance as they are asked to think about their writing while moving. Although not the focus of this chapter, I will explore these moments when students experience feelings of internal resistance to embodied writing pedagogy. I will reflect on why I, as a teacher-researcher, observed such resistance as meaningful and indicative of intellectual growth for my students as writers. To use a metaphor with embodied origins, if what challenges us changes us, then my student writers who felt most challenged by embodied writing were the ones most hesitant and less metacognitively attuned to their physical bodies' connections to the writing process. For most of this chapter, though, I focus on student writers who benefited from embodied writing activities because writing pedagogues ought to be interested in how the role of the body shapes a student's writing experience.

The student writers whose voices I feature in this chapter come to us from two different studies conducted at two equally different universities in Texas. The first group of writers I studied were enrolled in a themed section of first-year composition taught at Texas Christian University (TCU). This course, English 10803T: Yoga-Zen Writing, was piloted in spring 2015. Initially, I developed the course to study how embodied writing strategies might improve students' regular writing practice and overall sense of physical and academic well-being.[28] The third and fourth students' experiences I will discuss are those of two advanced undergraduate English majors enrolled in my fall 2019 English 4473: Freelance Writing course at Texas Woman's University (TWU). I developed this course based on my past experiences as a freelance writer for several magazines and newspapers. I had the audacious goal of getting some of our students published in local news and lifestyle media outlets.[29]

From May, 2015, to December, 2019, I collected writing samples from student writers in the form of journal entries, blog posts, submitted papers, and (for some classes) daily writing logs for the two courses that incorporate acts of embodied writing. After completing all necessary data collection and using my research questions as a framework, I read the data first, and then I began coding for themes that arose from the data using a grounded theory approach.[30] By the time this first round of data collection was complete, I found myself transitioning workplaces, from TCU to TWU in the summer of 2018. Working at a new university provided me with a drastically different student demographic but less drastic differences in terms of my findings. At TCU, in 2015 approximately 60% of students enrolled identified as female and 40% identified as male (TCU Office of Institutional Research). However, in my TCU Yoga-Zen Writing section, 84% of the students enrolled in my spring

2015 section were female, and all of the students were traditional-aged college students (aged eighteen to twenty-two). In contrast, at TWU in fall 2019, 86% of undergraduate students were female and 14% were male, and this was adequately well represented in my Freelance Writing course, where out of nineteen students, three identified as male, fourteen identified as female, and two identified as non-gender conforming. All nineteen students were traditional college-aged students, but the ethnic demographic of this second group was notably more diverse than the former group. Whereas TCU is a predominantly white institution (72%) and my Yoga-Zen Writing students were also predominantly white, TWU is a minority-majority serving institution that has nearly as many Hispanic students (31.4%) as white students (36.6%).[31] More than half of my TWU Freelance Writing course students were white (52%), however, and Hispanic (21%), African-American (11%), and Asian (11%) students constituted a smaller overall minority.[32] Approximately half of TWU students are first-generation college students and 44% qualify as Pell Grant eligible. My purpose in providing institutional data on both of these universities is to give a snapshot of the student demographics seen in these two very different classrooms.

EMBODIED WRITING STUDENTS

English 10803T: Yoga-Zen Writing

English 10803T: Yoga-Zen Writing is a themed section of a general education writing course requirement taken primarily by first-year students at TCU. My interest in designing this course stemmed from an experience I had at a Wring-and-Write Workshop at a studio in Fort Worth, Indigo Yoga, during which I and almost a dozen other women journaled about ideas for writing projects between short, twenty-minute yoga sessions. During this workshop, there was laughter and there were tears and encouraging words as the participants shared their struggles with eating disorders, infertility, alcoholism, and multiple sclerosis. The integration of physical movement seemed to help the participants tap into a deeper awareness of their bodies, bodily issues, and embodied writing processes. I wanted to bring this embodied awareness to my own writing students, so the course I designed centered around yoga and included yoga sequences. Throughout the semester, I planned approachable, adaptable yoga sequences for my students. The sequence of instruction on our "yoga days," as the students called them, usually included a "Warm Up," or an introduction to the content we were to cover that day, followed by me posing an exploratory question, followed by instruction through several poses, breaks to write, more flowing through yoga poses, and one or more additional breaks to write. On days when my students did not practice yoga in class, they were encouraged to tap into their understanding of yoga to make meaningful learning connections between the practice of yoga and the practice of writing. To do so, students completed journal entries in class each week, sometimes twice each week, whenever we needed to reflect on a particular meditation, yoga practice, supplementary reading, or a general question related to our writing processes.

In the course, the student learning outcomes guided instruction to ensure that students were introduced to a range of genres and instructed on how to use rhetorical conventions within those genres to improve their ability to read and cite sources with a critical lens, to employ flexible revision and drafting strategies, and ultimately to understand writing as a recursive process. As the predecessor to English 20803: Writing as Argument, this course prepared students to learn about writing strategies and practices more generally before focusing on the methods of persuasive writing to be learned in their next writing course. Much of this writing was conducted in a communal-feeling computer lab classroom that was lined with Dell desktop computers and provided enough seating in the center of the room for each of the twenty students to sit at a large conference room-style table made up of six smaller tables. My lectern computer backed up to a floor-to-ceiling whiteboard wall that doubled as a projection screen, and with three walls of windows the classroom benefited from plenty of sunlight. When we needed more floor space to roll out our yoga mats, everyone helped move the center tables toward the back of the room. These quarters were cramped, but we had just enough room for every student to lay down in savasana pose—a final resting pose to be taken at the end of practice—without being head-to-toe in the most literal sense.

After the course ended, I reviewed over 700 pages of writing samples submitted by these students, which included weekly journal entries that promoted freewriting and association strategies for reflecting on their work as writers, casual blog posts geared toward an audience of readers or writers who may be interested in exploring embodied writing habits, and formal paper assignments—occasionally accompanied by author's memorandums or other forms of reflective writing. In the syllabus, I explained that these entries might be thought of as opportunities to focus on informal process work to build self-discipline, as a writer, and to gain respect for embodied practices, such as yoga and mindfulness, intended to support writerly development. I also underscored the need to avoid rushing to complete a "finished product," asking students to take time to be reflective in journal entries.

Blog asanas were another low-stakes writing assignment featured in this course. Twice for each writing challenge and twice for the final assignment, students produced 350- to 500-word blog posts. In yoga, an asana is a position or posture that brings about a certain energetic effect within the practitioner. The use of the term *blog asana* connected to our course theme and encouraged students to think about writing activity as a kind of physical activity—at least while the idea was fresh in their minds in the beginning. Ten asanas were submitted in total and they were always due before the start of class. The purpose of designing regular writing practice opportunities was threefold: first, to prepare the student for class discussion; second, to generate ideas for their own writing through analytical thinking; and third, to practice writing brief analysis papers common in academic writing one will do in college. Asanas were uploaded to the students' chosen blogging platforms, which I helped each student create toward the beginning of the course. In total, the ten asanas accounted for twenty percent of my students' total grades.

For readings, students read selections of text from Bruce Ballenger's *The Curious Writer*, Gerald Graff and Cathy Birkenstein's *They Say, I Say*, and well-known restorative yoga scholar Judith Lasater's book, *Living Your Yoga*. Readings from *The Curious Writer* assisted students with the learning of genre conventions, while Graff and Birkenstein's book supported students in understanding the tone of academic writing in a more general sense. Lasater's book was a keystone text for helping students see the ways in which yoga and meditation practices transcend physical contexts, demonstrating how such practices come to bear on everyday living and working tasks, of which writing is no exception. For many journal entries and blog asanas, students were asked to connect the teachings of *Living Your Yoga* to existing knowledge of the writing process set forth by composition scholars.

The accrued amount of physical movement in a course that connects writing to yoga can vary greatly—and should vary depending on an instructor's comfort level with teaching embodied writing as well as an intake assessment of students' ability levels and needs. When I first taught this course in 2015, I dedicated only three class periods to the extended exploration of yoga, and I recruited local yoga teachers with different approaches to the teaching of yoga to teach my students. Other class periods featured shorter, yoga-inspired stretching breaks and mindfulness meditation practices so that almost every class period featured some sort of contemplative movement or sensorimotor reflection. In course evaluations, quite a few students requested more class periods dedicated to the practice of yoga. When I taught this themed course again in Fall 2016, I allotted five class periods to extended yoga sessions, which included more questions for journal writing that pertained to student writing specifically. I also taught the yoga sessions myself to improve the consistency of the yoga practices my students experienced, an action I would not have taken with the previous students because I had not yet begun my 200-Hour Yoga Alliance Registered Teacher Training course.

Careful navigation of the classroom space and teacher participation within that space can greatly enhance the learning experiences of students. In each of the three yoga sessions held for my spring 2015 students, I introduced key learning points for the day's yoga class and lesson on writing, followed by an introduction to our guest yoga teacher, the yoga practice itself, and the questions for reflection at the end of the class. Students were asked to bring a towel or yoga mat to practice on. For the first session, the class was able to move most of the desks to the sides of the room, but the closeness at which students had to practice next to one another was a little too close to be comfortable. For the second and third yoga sessions, I was able to secure a spacious studio room in the basement of our university's recreation center, which provided mats to all students, clean hardwood floors, and mirrors in which they could watch themselves move. For these later two sessions, I created handouts that highlighted key reflection points and questions for the day's session. The guest teachers were responsive to the physical needs and limitations of every student, making poses more accessible by offering modifications, when needed, and I practiced the movements with my students. My intention for practicing both the yoga movements and responding to the questions I posed was to demonstrate to students that these actions have potential beyond the classroom. As a professional writer who shares my journalistic and academic work with students from time to time, I strive to model my own writing strategies and to discuss my own embodied writing experiences with my students when appropriate. Rather than an observer, I seek to be a participant in the collective embodied writing experience of the class. I believe my modeling and my participation in embodied writing experiences increased my rapport with students as their teacher and fostered a sense of trust in them. By moving and writing alongside them, I came to know several of these student writers very well. In the next sections, I introduce two students enrolled in my TCU Yoga-Zen Writing class,: Vanessa and LeAnna. After some discussion of each of these first two profiles of students with strong restorative thinking preferences, I will discuss the relevance of rest to creative work before segueing to the final two profiles of students enrolled in my TWU Freelance Writing class.

Vanessa

Raised in sunny California, Vanessa was a slender young woman with long, light brown hair in tightly curled ringlets that were pulled back into a ponytail holder on most days. Her eagerness to discuss yoga and her calm but can-do attitude made her one of the most active participants in our class that semester. Vanessa was also, by far, the most experienced (and enthusiastic) yoga practitioner of all the students in the spring 2015 course. Though other students had tried yoga once or twice before our class—several students had never tried yoga—Vanessa had been to many different kinds of yoga classes, and this experience explains why she remained noticeably more open-minded to embodied writing than many of her peers when it came to trying new poses or styles of meditation. She sat up front, close to my right side every day. She participated actively, frequently raising her hand to answer yoga- or writing-related questions posed to the class. Inasmuch as she was willing to engage with the content of the course, Vanessa remained somewhat guarded at times, revealing small details about her personal life or what brought her to practice yoga in a most elusive way at the beginning of the semester, hinting at a deeper purpose or attachment to the practice of yoga every once in a while.

Vanessa's background in yoga and her enthusiasm for the physical movements of yoga make her an exceptional example of how—under optimal conditions and circumstances—students can be open to and benefit from embodied writing practices. In her first journal entry for the semester, recorded on January 15, 2015, Vanessa was prompted to write in response to the following questions: "Have you ever tried yoga? Liked it? Hated it? Why is that? How do you feel about it now? How could it impact your writing experience?" In her response, she shared how and why she came to practice yoga:

> Yoga has recently become an important part of my life—about a year ago, I began to become interested in the practice of yoga (at the time, for the physicality of the practice). I took some classes here and there, but nothing too extreme. Over the summer, I began SculptYoga and became more passionate about the entirety of the yoga practice, not just the "working out" aspect of it. When my anxiety got to its worst, I turned to yoga for help and the results have been (so far) tremendous. I now have a deep yearning to learn/ practice more of the mental side of yoga, as well as to continue the practice!

Bringing remarkable background knowledge and past experiences to our class, Vanessa quickly became known in class as one of the most willing and exuberant student advocates of embodied writing pedagogy. In this way, she was an exception, not the norm. Although several other students had previously been practitioners of yoga or had articulated an enthusiasm to learn more about yoga and meditation, Vanessa was by far the most engaged student. I am showcasing her experiences as an outstanding example of what is possible when students bring sincere interest and open-mindedness to a course that unites physical activity and writing activity.

As noted in Bazerman and Tinberg's definition of embodied cognition, the affective aspects or emotions tied to embodiment can play a significant role in the writing processes of writers. What was also interesting about Vanessa was her casual mention of anxiety. When people say they have anxiety, they may be referring to a clinical diagnosis that requires daily medication, or they may be referring to anxiety as a feeling of restlessness or unwarranted worrying about situations and outcomes beyond their control. I refrained from asking Vanessa to explain what her anxiety entailed, but as the semester wore on she revealed more about her anxiety and how it affected her writing practice. In her first writing challenge, for example, she wrote a narrative-style personal essay about a mantra that defines how she lives her life: "I choose to be healthy in mind, body, and soul." In her essay, she describes her life as a content, healthy high school student whose "pen was furiously scribbling, each and every day, writing my story." She did not clarify what she meant by "her story," but from out-of-class conversations I learned that she had previously been an avid journaler, one who deeply enjoyed her writing classes. What followed this statement was an explanation as to why this personal decision mattered so much to her:

> But something changed. Towards the end of high school, I began to make choices that were more harmful than helpful to my mind, body, and soul. I quickly lost sight of who I was as a person, straying from everything around me. I lost myself in a whirlwind of substance abuse, choosing temporary happiness over the beautiful life I had before me. It wasn't long before my pen slowly stopped writing; I no longer had time to write my story, nor did I want to. I put my pen down and wandered off.

The euphemistic way Vanessa writes about past experiences with addiction challenges was a trademark unique to her. As a writing teacher, it would be inappropriate for me to ask a student to volunteer more information than what they have already shared about their history of substance abuse, so I did not press Vanessa to write in more depth and detail about what troubled her. What I can gather from what Vanessa has shared, though, is that her emotions are closely tied to her embodied writing practice. Laura Micciche is one scholar who has called for more attention to the role of emotion in the writing classroom, and in her book, *Doing Emotion: Rhetoric, Writing, Teaching*, she has specifically stated the ways in which embodiment and emotion intertwine. Illuminating Micciche's claims, Vanessa reiterates the significance of emotion and embodiment as she begins to make sense of the relationship between physical activity and writing activity from an undergraduate student writer's perspective.

Long before I landed on the term restorative thinking to name what I was watching unfold in embodied writing classes, I was simply curious about Vanessa's interest in yoga as a conduit through which her embodied writing practices could take shape. Clearly identifying as an embodied writer from early on in the semester, Vanessa's reflective writing continued to shed light on how she viewed the relationship between the physical activity of our class and her extracurricular yoga endeavors. For our first in-class yoga session in January, 2015, I asked, "How does your body/ mind feel today?" Vanessa responded to the first question by saying, "Not steady/comfortable today: my energy/focused (tired!)." Her post-yoga writing reflection contrasted with this statement quite a bit. She was asked, "How does your mind or your body feel now? What's different or similar? What questions do you have about this in-class activity?" She responded as follows:

After the yoga, my *mind* feels amazing. My body feels more open, but still hurts a bit . . . but my mind feels entirely cleansed and open. Not as tired, not as uncomfortable.

Living Your Yoga = You can live yoga and I think this is true. Like our mantras, we can put to action words or phrases (healthy M/B/S). I can live out my dreams and encouragements.

Questions: - Can we do more yoga in this class? I loved today! - When did you start doing yoga?

In this entry, there are a few embodied cognition concepts at play. First, Vanessa makes a clear distinction between how she felt tired or lethargic prior to our yoga session and how she feels as though she has entered an improved mental state of clarity after doing yoga in class. I commonly read student responses reflecting on how relaxed and clear-headed they feel after engaging in our yoga-writing sessions. In a later journal entry, Vanessa describes our yoga session with a local yoga studio owner and teacher as "much needed with finals coming up" because her mind longed for a chance to "just relax and take a break," an opportunity she would not have afforded herself had it not been required of her for our course. In both entries, we see the onset of restorative thinking. That is, student writers, like Vanessa, embrace these in-class opportunities to step away from the demands of knowledge-making for the purposes of academic writing and instead refocus their attention on a physical activity that restores the mind after undergoing the cognitive demands of writing or the rigors of other academic work, thereby preparing her to return to her writing work with fresh focus and enthusiasm. Her journal entry could be read as an experience marked by restorative thinking because she is also alleviating a mental burden she had come to class with—one that caused her cognitive fatigue but allowed her to unload what burdened her in preparation for writing. Restorative thinking supports a student writer, like Vanessa, providing a strategic release in the form of a physical activity.

Interestingly enough, in this last excerpt from Vanessa's writing we can see that she is capable of engaging in knowledge structuring at the time she wrote this entry. Just before her friendly request for more yoga time in class, Vanessa also makes a rather raw attempt at knowledge structuring. She alludes to the title of our supplementary reading material in *Living Your Yoga*, proffering that the mental clarity yoga provides can be translated into everyday living. Interestingly, Vanessa chooses to connect an example of everyday living to her writing. She sees the way in which "we can put into action words or phrases," as she claims to have accomplished in the writing challenge that focused on the topic of connecting a healthy mind to a healthy body and soul. Here, she is enacting knowledge structuring, or applying a way of organizing information (i.e., a knowledge structure, a cognitive structure connecting physical activity to writing activity—a sort of edifying action that builds new pathways for understanding). Vanessa is making the connection between bringing the clarity that comes with the physical practice of yoga into everyday living as that pertains to enacting a spoken and written mantra, specifically.

Of the ten blog asanas assigned to students this semester, the ninth proved to be the most interesting in terms of reflecting on embodied writing strategies because each student was asked to take an asana break, as inspired by Christy Wenger's "Yoga Asana Handout: Iyengar Yoga for Writers." This handout is provided in the appendices of Wenger's book, *Yoga Minds, Writing Bodies*, and it offers writers simple, accessible yoga poses to assume at various points during a writing session. The sequence of poses began with a simple standing pose, called Mountain Pose, which was illustrated by Wenger in the handout. For this pose, students were asked to "Set an intention to their practice." and to "Bring attention to the breath." (199). The next poses in the handout, Tree Pose and Triangle Pose, are suggested for writers when they "get stuck, can't concentrate or need a break" (Wenger 199). Wenger offers half a dozen other poses that guide the writer through physical movements that support the writing process before recommending students end their writing session in repose, that is, on the floor in final relaxation pose, or savasana, which supports the writer's mind and body with a feeling of full acceptance of the writing session and frees any emotions felt during the process (201). For this blog asana, students were given the following prompt:

> Blog Asana 9: Before starting the more involved work of making a vlog, read through this activity from *Yoga Minds, Writing Bodies [hyperlinked]*. Now, begin your work as the activity directs. End your work as the activity directs, too, and pay attention to the moments when your work might benefit from the "asana solutions" the activity recommends. At the end of your working session, write to me (350–500 words) about how easy or difficult it was to implement these asana breaks. What might you

have done (or do) differently after trying these? Share any other insights you gain from this experience.

"As the activity directs" refers to the final writing challenge prompt my students received. Students were working on their final video blog asana (or "vlog") toward the end of the course when this handout was used. Vanessa responded to this assignment with the following:

> Implementing asana breaks into my work was actually one of the most beneficial things I could have done to improve my work habits. Before starting this assignment, I was tentative about taking breaks during my work—I do better without breaks in my work, as I find I get distracted or sidetracked if I do take a break. That being said, I was more open to the idea of taking a little asana break during my work because it implemented simple yoga poses that I knew wouldn't be too distracting. I began my work . . . as the sheet prompted, making sure to open my mind and prepare for the work ahead. I set an intention: to finish the study guide to the best of my ability. My mountain pose was strong and sturdy, and I hoped this would transfer over into my work for the evening. As I began the study guide, I noticed myself tensing up at times I did not know an answer fully or had to check for an answer in my book. I took these moments of weakness to start an asana break, to regroup my mind and refocus. The breaks were actually invigorating; I was able to collect myself and refocus on the assignment at hand. Typically, I just try to work through the distraction/pain, which often results in a mediocre final outcome. These asana breaks helped me to produce the best possible work I could, because both my body and my mind were at ease with the entire process. I think these asana breaks should be implemented more regularly into our daily schedules, as I am sure they can help us on more levels than one. If we start and finish our daily tasks with a more open and receptive mind/body, we are able to put our best self forward and produce our best work possible. All in all, I think I will definitely be implementing this practice into my daily life!

The overwhelming majority of statements made by Vanessa in this post reveal that she thinks of these asanas as restorative in nature or a way to cognitively ease the difficult work of writing. She uses words such as "refocus," "at ease," and "open and receptive," all of which are demonstrative of restorative thinking. Clearly, when Vanessa takes asana "breaks," she is taking them to release her mind from writing, not to generate new ideas for writing while undergoing a physical transition to a new pose. Here I want to recognize the fact that a concept like bodily uptake could apply to what a student experiences, but the restorative nature of Vanessa's description shows that she is not uptaking knowledge of her physical body for the sake of generating new knowledge. Her engagement is markedly restorative and points to an example of how the concept of bodily uptake is too narrow to include other ways of embodied knowing.

Christy Wenger on Restorative Thinking. Although yoga is a physical practice that can support both generative and restorative thinking, Wenger confirms that her students frequently use yoga poses as justifiable "breaks" from writing rather than opportunities to continue writing. For Wenger, moments of generative thinking occur at times when she experiences a "creative burst" in her writing while "doing something very physical," which for her includes yoga, running, and CrossFit workouts. An axiom of her argument in *Yoga Minds, Writing Bodies* centers on her belief that sensorimotor movement and meditation practices can help writers create new ideas, not just restore minds after long writing sessions. Her pedagogical history of teaching students to connect their yoga movements to writing processes has made clear to her, however, that students prefer yoga practices to function as opportunities for restorative thinking, also known as "yoga breaks."

As a leading expert in embodied writing, Wenger has taken an earnest interest in student writers' affinity for restorative thinking. During our interview, Wenger went on to explain how students view yoga movement as breaks from writing. She said,

> I hear my students say, "yoga breaks." That's what they call it. I think that's just how we think of it, like we're either working or we're getting time to play. So, when we're working, we're at the computer working. But when we're doing yoga, we're playing. And so, they think about it as breaks, and that's not necessarily a bad thing. But for me, personally, and what I see with my students is that there's something transformative again about the experiences we're returning to, like we're doing this and coming back to the task, and so it creates a circle where they're kind of interconnected. . . . It's not like one of them you can just leave behind.

Wenger confirms what Vanessa and other students' reflective writing makes clear: Student writers see physical movement in the classroom as an opportunity for restorative thinking, not generative thinking. She clarifies that she does not think this is a "bad thing" or in any way detrimental to their development as writers. Given the confines of the college writing classroom, the limitations of space needed to move, and the sometimes slower, more meditative postures of a yoga practice, it makes sense that students would view yoga movements as "yoga breaks," as opposed to "yoga brainstorming sessions" or "yoga think time." A physical exercise that requires more rapid movement, such as running, would cause students to generate more new ideas for writing due to the faster heart rate and breaths taken per minute. If too much rapid movement and exertion is required, however, the mind cannot function as well (Aitchison et al.). Still, these breaks have the potential to be "transformative," according to Wenger, and dynamically "interconnect[ing]" writing activity to physical activity. Therefore, the students need not be thinking about these physical movements as a way to generate new knowledge about their writing or thinking about their writing at all. Instead, a "yoga break," a run, a mindful walk, or a secular mindfulness meditation session can provide opportunities for students to leave their writing at their desks and return to that work with fresh minds. Whether or not students choose to generate knowledge during physical activity is entirely dependent on the student's interest and ability, or a matter of conscious control, dependent on the kind of work the student is doing, and quite possibly a result of how much free time the student builds into their schedule to move, to meditate, to relax, or to restore in other productive, healthy ways that benefit their minds as writers.

LeAnna

As the first person in her family to pursue higher education, LeAnna was raised by her single father in San Antonio, a place of origin she mentioned frequently in class discussions. She was a Latinx student of petite build with thick, smooth and straight tresses that seemed to stay perfectly in place throughout class, even as she made sudden, sometimes jerky movements to express herself from her chair when she felt she could not find her voice to articulate her frustrations with society at times. Despite being fairly shy, LeAnna wrote far more expressively than most students, writing often about what challenged her emotionally and physically, revealing a bit more each week about the personal hardships she faced, and occasionally connecting those experiences to embodied writing experiences. For example, she frequently struggled to reconcile her progressive beliefs with the more conservative, white, privileged opinions of her classmates, an occurrence that prompted her to research and write about activist issues for several of her writing challenge papers in our course. I remember days when she could talk cheerily with her classmates and other days when she could hardly hide her disapproval of her peers' opinions. By the end of our semester together, she decided to transfer to a university closer to her hometown. Nevertheless, she worked diligently to end her semester on a personally meaningful note, even winning a contemplative poetry contest sponsored by TCU's undergraduate journal, *eleven40seven,* for a poem that explored her feelings about her mental health.

The ability to engage with restorative thinking instead of generative thinking is often a matter of intention or conscious control. LeAnna, like so many student writers, is capable of consciously controlling her thoughts about writing while moving, even if it feels unnatural to her at first. Recall the second in-class yoga day journal prompt detailed in my analysis of Vanessa, the one in which I asked students what took courage for them to do in their yoga practice and in their writing practice as two distinct, separate questions. In LeAnna's journal, she began with a short paragraph reminding me that the practice of yoga always challenges her sense of physical control followed by a paragraph that connects her yoga practice to her writing practice:

> It was hard to start at first, as it always is. Especially since I haven't practiced in a very long time. But I found that with each breath, I was getting more relaxed and more in tune with myself.
>
> This kind of relates to my writing. I start off very hesitant, afraid to start off unorganized, so I kind of end up staring at the screen/ paper until something comes to mind, but once I've got it, I can go on forever.

LeAnna directly relates her yoga practice to her writing practice even though the connection did not need to be directly made. Or in the case of some students, a connection exists between writing activity and physical activity, but this connection need not be described or mentioned to fulfill this simple writing assignment. LeAnna, however, refers to the connection when she says, "This kind of relates to my writing." What follows is a series of descriptors that define her writing most obviously but could also define her previously assessed yoga practice. She describes how she feels "hesitant, afraid to start off unorganized," and how, when she finally does begin, she feels warmed up enough that she could "go on forever." Both statements indicate that she views writing and yoga as activities making use of similar processes. This description epitomizes knowledge structuring. With language, LeAnna builds a structure that could be applied to understand either writing or yoga as similar processes and through which she feels she can come to understand the other in a different way. From my perspective as someone who has been writing professionally for over a decade and who has been reflecting on the relationship between physical activity and writing activity for just as long, I marvel at how her use of this particular knowledge structure is different from how I used knowledge structures in Chapter Two to convey my history of connecting physical activity to writing activity. Although students may be less adept at creating knowledge structures than professional writers, the possibilities for enriching student learning about writing with knowledge structures are limitless. If we can integrate discussions about the value of conscious control over one's physical activity and writing activity, then we can begin to see more students benefiting from knowledge structuring.

Because many students feel challenged by the act of consciously controlling their physical activity and writing activity, mindful walking exercises can be a helpful supplementary activity for students. I will share one more example of LeAnna's writing, a snippet that provides greater insight into the mind of a student writer exploring generative or restorative thinking through this course I designed. For my students' sixth blog asana, I gave them the following directions:

WALK WITH AN IDEA

First, complete our readings for tomorrow. . . . Then, I want you to go for a walk.

Yes, you're going to walk, but before you start walking, write in your journal a few lines about your initial reactions to the writing of those two bloggers. Did you like their writing? Dislike their writing?

Next, plan your walking path. The path should take you about ten to fifteen minutes, ending at a calm place where you can sit with your legs crossed. Bring pen, paper, or your laptop with you.

The purpose of this asana was to introduce my students to other forms of contemplative movement. Besides yoga and seated styles of meditation, mindful walking, sometimes known as walking meditations, can support a thinker or writer in the creation of new knowledge or the restoration of cognitive capability before or after a writing session begins. In a speech originally delivered at Munich University in 1918, Max Weber unveiled how new ideas occur to him while walking. He declared that

> Ideas occur to us when they please, not when it pleases us. The best ideas do indeed occur to one's mind in the way in which Ihering describes it: when smoking a cigar on the sofa; or as Helmholtz states of himself with scientific exactitude: when taking a walk on a slowly ascending street; or in a similar way. In any case, ideas come when we do not expect them, and not when we are brooding and searching at our desks. (Weber 6)

Weber's assessment of walking up a steep hill to generate new ideas will feel relatable for some writers, but not all writers need to trek up a steep incline to get extra blood flowing to their brains. The repetitive motion of walking on flat ground in any direction appears to be more than enough movement to light up different creative centers in the brain. In fact, a series of four experiments conducted by experimental psychologists at Stanford University in 2014 shows that "walking boosts creative ideation in real time and shortly after" (Oppezzo and Schwartz 1142). Additionally, these same experiments showed that participants experienced a residual creative boost while seated after a walk, and that walking outside produced "the most novel and highest quality analogies" in contrast to other walking simulations, including walking inside, on a treadmill inside, or being pushed in a wheelchair outside (Oppezzo and Schwartz 1142). Almost all of my students chose to walk outside, away from campus, some sharing with me that they did not want to be seen by their friends while wandering aimlessly or having to stop and talk to people on campus or on the track at our campus recreation center. When assigning this activity in class, I encouraged students to think about their walks like their meditations, to use breathing patterns we learned in class, such as taking four short breaths in and four short breaths out in a continuous pattern and in sync with each footfall, or to pay attention to their breath in another mindful way.

How or where writers walk might be as important to the creative process as why they walk. In a 2016 study conducted by educational psychologists, researchers in Switzerland set out to study the effects of free walking—meaning walking in any direction—as opposed to rectangular walking—ambling in a rectangular pattern, of course—and they found that free walking improved the creative thinking abilities of both younger and older adults (Kuo 1580). Composition studies scholars should consider how the act of walking leads to more creative thinking about one's writing. This embodied cognition connection gives scholars reason to pause and consider the ways in which the simple, natural movement of walking benefits student writers during their time studying at universities and later in life when they move into a professional career trajectory, such as professional writing or other fields requiring creative endeavor.

LeAnna experienced a creative burst while partaking in her walking meditation, but she makes no secret as to how challenged she feels by generative thinking. In her thoughtful, somewhat metaphorical reflection, she begins with the addition of a new idea: that "there's always a destination." LeAnna wrote:

> *"Walk the Thought"*
>
> Here's the thing about walking: there's always a destination. I can't remember the last time I had wandered around aimlessly, until today of course. I chose to do this at night to avoid a crowd of people—I like the quiet. Taking steps without thinking about the walking itself was pretty easy, but walking and thinking about a specific idea? That was a little harder. Physically wandering made my mind want to wander as well. Trying to focus on two blogs I read before I started moving was like trying to read a serious book while listening to a stand-up comedy special by Gabriel Iglesias. I had to remind myself that my mind had a destination even though my feet didn't.

This paragraph is the first of three paragraphs in her asana, and this one is perhaps the best example of student preference for restorative thinking I have read. Undoubtedly, she realizes that she needs to be generating new ideas about writing, but she is met with a feeling of resistance toward being generative and of preference for the freedom that restorative thinking allows. Clearly, to "walk the thought" challenges her sense of control as a student writer. Requiring her to walk—even aimlessly, as in free walking, not patterned or mapped walking—and to think about the writing of others gave her a sense of cognitive overload. For her, wandering as a walker made her "mind want to wander as well." Her unfocused movement made her feel cognitively unfocused on the writing task at hand, but it also shows her engagement with conscious control. Her analogy illustrates that both require her to pay attention to the acts of walking and thinking, as one wants to pay attention to a "serious book" or "Gabriel Iglesias," but thinking about her final destination or purpose for this writing activity gave her some sense of focus, however small that could be. This paragraph also demonstrates that generative thinking and knowledge structuring were not easily available to LeAnna at the outset of this embodied writing activity. If she had been able to generate new knowledge while walking as easily as our professional writers had, then we would have read about how she came across new ideas or garnered new insights for her sixth blog asana. Without a doubt, she makes apparent her struggle to engage in generative thinking, and she explains in descriptive terms how her acclimation to a state of conscious control challenges her.

Eventually, walking made it easier for LeAnna to regain control over her writing. In her second paragraph, her experience changes. She writes that

> After a while, . . . my thoughts started to catch up. The background noise in my head slowly faded out, although I wasn't able to completely silence them. Instead of trying to quietly verbalize and organize my reaction to some blogs and a reading on control, I started to visualize them. I saw color and blurs of shapes clouding together, giving me a sense of reflection. It's challenging to articulate this experience, so bear with me. It was more about feeling my reaction than scripting them – needless to say it was weird. When I found a place that felt like a good resting point, I crossed my legs and stared at nothing. Controlling the mind over controlling the body, I concluded, is what leads to success. Yes, health is important, but people forget that exercising the mind is just as important. Learning to focus and center on whatever you need at the moment goes hand in hand with listening to your intuition—a path many spiritual people interpret as strong, and the "right" way to live life.

This paragraph in LeAnna's writing represents a clear shift in creative perspective. She goes from struggling to think about her writing and moving at the same time to finding a way to control consciously her thinking about her writing in terms of "color and blurs of shapes." Her deeply visual cognition strategy helped her feel her reaction to the writing assignment instead of "scripting" a false or untrue assessment of the pieces of writing she was asked to reflect on. When she states that it was "challenging to articulate this experience," she signals to me that embodied cognition is taking place. Embodied cognition is markedly difficult to describe for writers who are new, inexperienced, or deeply unaware of their bodies and how those bodies can benefit their writing work. In the case of LeAnna, we see someone who has reported struggling with body image in classroom yoga sessions and who shares her struggles with this walking meditation at the beginning of this writing assignment. Eventually, however, she focuses her mind while walking with visualization of the writing texts she was assigned to read, and she felt her reaction to them before finding a resting point at which she could stop and collect the thoughts she had generated. Notice how I wrote *generated*, once again, to denote that she is making new knowledge at this point in her walking meditation. She is moving her body physically while thinking, and she seems to know that using both activities together will unlock some kind of creative potential she cannot yet understand at the outset of her walk. Instead, she trusts the process, she takes the walk, she tries a new cognition strategy to help herself collect her thoughts while she moves, and then she finds that strategy works for her. She is able to generate new knowledge, which defines the theme of this blog asana that I will paraphrase in more concrete terms: mindless walking and mindless writing will get you to the wrong destination. Like the poet Thomas Gardner, when LeAnna uses physical movement to regain control of her mind, she attempts to regain control of her writing process. The astute conclusion she comes to is evidence of how powerful this embodied cognition strategy can be.

The perceived cognitive challenge of controlling the mind by controlling the body's physical activity seems daunting, but it is, in fact, intellectually meaningful to students. Students perceive generative thinking and knowledge structuring as requiring more critical thinking on the part of the writer than restorative thinking. It would make sense that student writers enrolled in required first-year writing classes, few of whom plan to be professional writers, would be less interested in engaging with the cognitively demanding task of generative thinking because the process of writing feels unfamiliar or difficult enough as is without requiring students to engage in additional knowledge-making (i.e., generative thinking) as a way of reflecting on the writing process. Regardless of whether or not this claim is true in the majority of student cases, we should not rule out the possibility that our students should be nudged toward generative ways of thinking while engaged in the writing process, especially in terms of embodied writing pedagogy. Consider the last of the three paragraphs LeAnna wrote for asana six:

> This ties into writing. Writing with a plan—an organized out-line—can only get you so far. It might lead to a good grade, but what does that really do for you? Are you actually learning? For me, I realized that focusing on the motions, the academic rou-tine, is terribly boring and pointless. I got a good enough grade . . . hooray? I did all of this hard work to reach this destination, but I still don't feel that I accomplished anything that really matters to me. I realized that writing aimlessly is the equivalent to going with my own flow and following a focused general idea instead of a structure that was laid out for me in a class-room. Sorting things out to fit that structure will get the de-sirable grade, but the path should be about reaching your own reflective point rather than something that might impress your educator. Dazzling your peers and your teachers is pretty cool, but surprising yourself is much, much more rewarding.

In this example, LeAnna demonstrates her ability to enact generative thinking by way of a knowledge structure she has created. In this blog post, which has become something of an extended metaphor, she has previously established how she connects writing to walking. By the end of her metaphor, we understand more clearly how walking without a destination can feel like writing with a script or a tight organizational structure that affords no creativity. She equates the final product, the good grade on the paper, with following academic guidelines and genre structures for writing, but writing freely is more personally rewarding to her. Likewise, she equates walking to meet a certain goal or in a cer-tain way to feel more mentally stifling than walking freely and welcom-ing the arrival of new ideas as they arise. Quite literally, she is building meaningful relationships between writing and walking, and this is what knowledge structuring looks like. If this were an instance of cognitive off-loading, she would not have grappled with her ideas on her walk at all. Instead, she would have set them aside to think about at a later time, and the walk would have served as a cognitively rejuvenating break from her writing. By doing the walk, she can do the talk, by which I mean that she has a novel idea to write about for having been challenged by connecting the physical act of writing to the cognitive act of thinking about her writing. By building this relationship, she has generated new knowledge that is personally meaningful to her writing process. And although she dislikes the cognitive challenge of having to grapple with her writing while walking with a focused mind, not a distracted one, what came of her focus was a new insight fueled by the residual creative boost gained from her walk.

Additionally, even seemingly aimless embodied movement supports students in achieving the aims of their writing tasks. I would liken LeAnna's assessment of academic writing to walking in a rectangular pattern. To be clear, I am not suggesting that academic writing has to be "terribly boring and pointless," as LeAnna has denounced such writing to be, but I do believe my students enjoyed exploring the loose, experimental genre of the blog post for these blog asanas because this style of writing invited them to take a break from the rigor and uniformity of academic writing. Modern Language Association style standards and the need to develop strong citation practices fit more with the rectangular pattern of walking that can stifle creativity but certainly do not have to under the right circumstances. Note, too, that throughout these three paragraphs LeAnna has not completely fulfilled the needs of the prompt, which asked her to assess and convey her thoughts on the writing of other blog writers. Regardless, I was pleased with what she shared. By walking aimlessly, and writing with even less aim, according to her, she arrived at an incredibly valuable conclusion about her own writing process and did so by way of embodied movement.

"The Rest" of Restorative Thinking. We ought to seriously consider the "rest" aspect of the writing process, and the value of restorative thinking as an effect. At this point, I want to pause in our analysis of student writers to introduce new and helpful research on the value of rest in the creative process. In December 2016, Stanford researcher Alex Soojung-Kim Pang published his latest book, *Rest: Why You Get More Done When You Work Less*, which draws on interdisciplinary research to establish the

benefits of rest in partnership with the benefits of work. In this text, Pang makes four claims:

> Claim 1: Work and rest are partners.

> Claim 2: Rest is active.

> Claim 3: Rest is a skill.

> Claim 4: Deliberate rest stimulates and sustains creativity. (11–15)

Few would disagree with Pang when he explains that work and rest are partners, I think, or at least that rest is required at times. More interesting to my research is the second claim: "Rest is active." Professional writer Christie Wright Wild used the concept of active rest to coach fellow writers on how to use running activity as a way of supporting their writing activity. In *Rest*, Pang makes a similar claim, saying that "[w]hen we think of rest, we usually think of passive activities: a nap, lying on the couch, watching sports on television, or binge-watching a popular TV series. That's one form of rest. But physical activity is more restful than we expect, and mental rest is more active than we realize" (12). In his book, he gives other, less physically rigorous examples of activities that stimulate active rest, such as painting or even staring into space. However, he frequently relies on physical exercise as the prime example of active rest. He even highlights the benefits of physical exercise as active rest for the work of creative people, such as writers:

> For a surprising number of creative people—including people in professions we usually think of as dominated by nerdy, bookish people who don't see the sun for weeks—strenuous, physically challenging, even life-threatening exercise is an essential part of their routine. Some walk miles every day or spend weekends working in their gardens. Some are always in training for the next marathon; others rock climb or scale mountains. Their idea of rest is more vigorous than our idea of exercise.
> So why is this restful? Serious exercise helps keep their bodies operating at their peak, which in turn keeps their minds sharp and gives them energy to do difficult work. (12–13)

As seen in the example of Thomas Gardner running six days a week or taking a simple stroll to his car after work, physical exercise as active rest need not be grueling to be effective. The health benefits are one outcome of physical exercise for creative people, but the mental relaxation this active rest provides is another underestimated benefit described in the fourth claim. But first, I want to add to his description of the third claim: "Rest is a skill." Pang compares the difficulty level of rest to "sex or singing or running," adding that when the rest is deliberate, it can actually help creative people "recover from the stresses and exhaustion of the day, allows new experiences and lessons to settle in your memory, and gives your subconscious mind space to keep working" (14). Instead of thinking of rest as a mindless or passive action to be taken, Pang nudges us to consider how quality rest requires more work than we realize. In fact, he explains in his "The Science of Rest" chapter that "one striking characteristic of the brain in its resting state is that it's barely less energetic than the engaged brain. Even when you're staring into space, your brain consumes only slightly less energy than it does when you're solving differential equations" (Pang 36). Rest is more active than we realize, and active in the sense that this time allows our brains to work on reclaiming space in our brains for continued cognitive function.

Pang does not call rest a strategy or even a kind of embodied cognition, but he writes along the same lines when he declares that the natural intelligence of the body can take over when the mind wearies from work. In the fourth claim, Pang states that "[d]eliberate rest stimulates and sustains creative activity" (15). In his depiction of this claim, he cites writers specifically: "Lots of great writers, scientists, and artists exercise regularly, and some are enthusiastic, accomplished athletes. They show an impressive consistency in habits and hobbies. They balance busy lives with deep play, forms of rest that are psychologically restorative, physically active, and personally meaningful" (Pang 16). The previous chapter on professional writers demonstrates that writers who engage with intensive physical training regimens, such as marathon training, purport to be generative thinkers primarily, but they also identified times when they allowed their minds to feel the more restorative effects of running or moving as needed. All of those participants demonstrated "impressive consistency" in so far as they had been able to maintain these levels of physical activity across several years, some logging their exercise patterns more consistently than others. I discussed the idea of consistency when I referenced Boice's excerpt on "Physical Conditioning" and the importance of exercise for the successful writer. Once again, we see how consistency or regularity in one's physical activity habits seems to benefit one's writing activity by way of embodied cognition strategies. For student writers, the opportunity to engage in active, deliberate rest seems to be even more important.

English 4473: Freelance Writing

In spring 2019, I was approached by my TWU department chair about the possibility of teaching a special topics course on freelance writing. Having an extensive background in freelance features journalism, I agreed without hesitation because I have always thought that English majors—at TWU and around the country—are equipped with superior composing and critical thinking skills, but so often they lack the preparation they need to advocate for their work in the competitive industries that writing and publishing have become. Assisting in the design of this course was TWU graduate student and first-year composition instructor, Margaret Williams, who prior to coming to TWU worked for decades as a news editor for Asheville, North Carolina's alternative newspaper *Mountain Xpress*—not to mention a dedicated practitioner of karate and tai chi. Our shared interest in embodiment motivated us to design a Writing + Wellness Log assignment, which prompted students to record their writing and exercise goals along with any relevant reflections on a daily basis for eight weeks (See Appendix A for a sample log template).

Of the nineteen students enrolled in the course, only one was of sophomore standing and the rest were upper-division English majors or minors. After the course ended in December, 2019, I read and coded through all logs and reflections on the logs to see if I could find any relevant references to embodied cognition's role in the writing process. More specifically, I looked for incidences where generative thinking, restorative thinking, or knowledge structuring were explored or suggested in student writing. I did not discuss these terms with students at any point during the course, but I did ask them to think about their personal wellness as writing and moving bodies. They read all of Joyce Carol Oates's *The Faith of a Writer* and wrote several discussion board posts on embodied writing content discussed within that book. We also incorporated opportunities for embodied movement within the class by taking movement breaks, which offered opportunities for the students to try tai chi, mindfulness meditations, walking meditations, and even theatrical-improvisational games. Twice in the semester, the Director of

TWU's Health and Well-Being Initiative visited our class to share re-sources and activities for them to work through the stress of academic writing. We wanted students to discuss healthy ways to reduce the in-ternal and external writing pressures they felt, especially as they thought about competing in the freelance writing industry, which tends to be a rather isolating experience at times. We tried to provide students with opportunities and resources that encouraged their thinking on the sub-ject of writing wellness and embodied cognition without giving them the technical terminology or framework we as researchers use to explain the common phenomena of generative thinking, restorative thinking, and knowledge structuring.

Mental well-being plays a starring role in every writer's creative pro-cess, and student writers are no exception. Worth noting here is that inasmuch as we sought to support the physical and mental well-being of these student writers, this semester greeted us and our students with some particularly difficult challenges, the hardest of which was the death of a faculty member in our department, Dr. Katie McWain. This tragedy sent seismic shock waves through my life, the lives of faculty and staff in our department, and the lives of our students especially. Our loss of Dr. McWain was reflected in the logs of students enrolled in this class, many of whom struggled with depression in the days and weeks that followed. Some students never spoke or wrote a word on their feel-ings about Dr. McWain's death, while others cried to us—the faculty and staff holed up in our downstairs offices—and gave hugs, delivered baked goods, became more comfortable sharing not only how their writ-ing was going but also how they were faring emotionally. Remnants of these difficult memories are preserved in those logs. When imagining this writing assignment to mirror that of which I originally designed for my professional writing study participants, I never would have thought that the dry and potentially even mundane genre of a writing log could become a daily reminder to check-in with one's mental health and writ-ing health. Surely, the logs may have seemed like a dull exercise to some students, but some of our freelance writing students in this particularly challenging semester really needed a space in which they could share in confidence to me what was and was not going well in their emotional, embodied, and writing processes. What the logs confirm for me, as a writing studies researcher, is that any embodied writing process can bring powerful emotions to the fore, an often-overlooked aspect of embodied writing that Laura Micciche and other writing scholars have identified in the past. For this reason and others, students were instructed to adapt writing logs to suit their individual needs as writers. One student added a new column to track her struggles with depression while another added a column to to help her convey the level of chronic pain she experienced on a given day. Like any movement practice, we recognized that we as writing instructors should encourage students to modify and adapt these logs to become the accessible instruments students need them to be; a one-size-fits-all approach would not suffice. In the next section, both of the freelance writing students' experiences came from those who completed robust and detailed logs in which they spoke to their emotional stress but not without making connections between their moving and writing processes.

Abbie

The first time I met Abbie in this class I was struck by her outgoing and forthcoming personality. Always eager to learn and to ask questions, she frequently talked to me about physical fitness. We bonded over our love of yoga and meditation, and we soon realized we were both planning to run in that year's Downtown Denton Turkey Trot 5K. Our embodied circumstances leading up to this footrace meant we both needed to train very differently. Abbie told me she was using every Tuesday and Thursday of the fall semester to train, and I, weeks away from my October 15 due date for my second son, remember telling her "I just want to finish." I hadn't run since August, and I only wanted to get through all 3.1 miles, whether that meant I running, walking, or crawling to the end.

On Thanksgiving Day, she spotted me in the corral, waiting to start. Never have I been able to meet up with a student runner-writer at a sanctioned running event. A different kind of pride filled me on that day, and as we crossed paths a few times in this event, I thought to myself, "I need to grade that stack of writing logs that's waiting for me at home."

In Abbie's writing logs, we see the innerworkings of restorative thinking as they unfold for a student writer. On the very first Monday of logging, Abbie met her daily movement goal of practicing yoga for twenty minutes and writing 1,461 words for her novel. In the reflections column of her log, she wrote of her mental health challenges, writing projects that were wearing her out, and on occasion, she reflected on her physical activity habits. What follows are a few excerpts from Abbie's log:

September 2, 2019: Was a little depressed, but felt better and clearer-headed after yoga. Reaching my goal and then some felt good.

September 5, 2019: Didn't feel my best. Depression sucks.

September 9, 2019: It's nice having a class mandating that I work out, otherwise I probably wouldn't be able to fit it in some days. Work is slow at the beginning of the semester, so I have more time for homework.

September 26, 2019: Things seem to be falling into place in my revision project . . . ? At least they'd better be. Biking gives me time to think about nothing, which I desperately need right now.

In some of these excerpts, Abbie is contextualizing her progress toward her physical and writing goals by sharing how her depression did or did not alter her plans for progress. Once again, emotions in student writing take center stage. Equally interesting are the small moments of reflection where she engages in restorative thinking. In the first reflection, she lets us know that she is still managing the nagging pull of lingering depression, but she credits a yoga practice as helping her clear her head of these feelings. Moving through yoga also helped her meet her writing goal for that day, which she noted to be a very specific 1,461 words and which she exceeded by a few hundred words. She comments on her revision project, one assigned for her capstone course that she agonizes over quite a bit in her logs, and she proclaims biking to be her creative vacuum for distancing herself from it. Internally, it seems that she experiences restorative thinking when she engages in various forms of physical activity.

The students' logs, although a useful mechanism for tracking individual progress toward physical activity and writing activity goals, did not allow for enough space to provide lengthier descriptions of their experiences with physical activity and writing activity. For this reason, I interviewed Abbie the following semester to talk to her about her experiences logging and engaging in embodied writing in our class. She let me know, very honestly, that she found the log frustrating at times. When the log was a mirror of her successes, logging felt affirmational, but not when the log forced her to record failed or incomplete attempts. When at the end of our interview I asked her if she sees a relationship between physical activity and writing activity, she said,

> For me, I typically turn to physical activity, especially when I'm depressed or anxious or just having a bad mental health day. I find that I struggle to put things into words when I have a bad mental health day, so by exercising I filter out the "mental blahs" . . . So, for me, running and exercise are a little more restorative rather than generative because I tend to focus more on how my body feels and how my mind feels in certain situations and certain problems. And then I'm able to come and sit back [at] my laptop and really focus, and put my thoughts into words because I've had time to push through everything, and wear my body out, and improve my attitude that way my mind feels better.

With this much longer exposition of Abbie's experience, we can see how emotional, physical, and creative toils swirl together to depict her process for restorative thinking. Abbie says that with exercise of any kind, particularly running, she "filter[s] out the 'mental blahs'" so that she can write. Worth noting is that Abbie only became familiar with the terms generative and restorative thinking in follow-up conversations with me after our course had ended. (I refrained from discussing these terms with students until writing logs had been submitted, the course had finished, and grades had been filed.) She also uses the terms restorative and generative to speak to her preference for restorative thinking quite directly. After our class ended, I continued to see Abbie at TWU's writing center, called the TWU Write Site, where she had worked as a tutor for several semesters. Prior to our follow-up interview, she had asked to interview me for a Write Site blog post on the connections between writing and running. In this post, which she cleverly titled, "Writing with Your Feet: The Creative Power of Running," she enlightens her readers about the benefits of writing and offers a little advice: "When stuck on a problem, one of the best solutions is to do something physically active. This allows our brains to rest from their mental work and forces us to concentrate on our physical bodies, and it is an effective solution to facing a mental block for several reasons." Here again, Abbie demonstrates her strong preference for running as a restorative thinking exercise that helps her overcome mental blocks. Running provides the active rest and recovery needed from the more taxing mental work of writing. Her recommendation of running to other writers for this purpose demonstrates that she is a firm advocate of running's role in the restorative thinking process.

Janna

Having taken Composition I and II with me during the 2018–2019 academic year, I was already very familiar with Janna's writing and her interest in physical activity. As the valedictorian of Denton High School and a top-placing swimmer in both freestyle and relay events, Janna was entering her second year of college with new personal goals: to publish her first novel and to compete in a triathlon. The semester took an unfortunate turn early on, however, when she re-injured her foot in a way that required surgery, taking her out of the triathlon training and putting her into crutches for several weeks. Nevertheless, Janna persisted in her writing goals—and the logging of those goals—despite feeling physically and mentally deterred by her injury. By the spring semester, she was in my office, smiling and handing me an autographed copy of her first published book, *Transforming Tears*, the true story of her grandfather's struggle to survive in British Malaya in the 1930s, now known as Malaysia, prior to immigrating to America.

Perhaps an equally generative and restorative thinker, Janna's diligent daily logging reveals her desire to run, even when she physically cannot, so she can write. Through her logging, she finds that on days when she exercises comfortably and safely she feels inspired to be more productive. Consider these four logging entries that document her reflections shortly after her surgery, which required several weeks of intensive physical therapy, culminating in her final entry for the very last day she logged:

> September 20, 2019: I have not been quite as active lately due to physical struggles and I think my mind knows and desperately wants to be able to get around more, however, I am still able to get things done but it does take much longer than usual, such as with this discussion post.

> October 14, 2019: I still feel as though I am just going through the motions in all that I am doing, even in my walks around campus because I would so prefer to run or be doing something more physically productive.

> October 18, 2019: Today's workout was the best because it's the first time in a couple of months that I have been able to get back to being this active, although I know I'm going to be really sore tomorrow. It will all be worth it and I even went back

to my hobby of creating bedtime stories and timing myself in how fast I can come up with and write a decent story from simply looking at a random image. I'd say today was the most efficient and productive day where my mind is actually present in a long while.

November 19, 2019: Reflecting back on most of this writing log and where I was to start, I feel as though I have come a long way through a recovery process as well and that says a lot. As for today, I was thinking of all this because of the more strenuous core workout I was doing and it made me realize that I would not be able to do this specific workout if it was earlier in the semester. I started thinking of processes overall, even in writing and that there are steps that have to be taken in order to get to where you want to be.

In the first entry, Janna discloses that her injury is disabling her body and her mind. The discussion post she refers to is one for our class, and writing this post has been prolonged past her usual time frame for writing discussion board posts because she cannot think as clearly without physical movement. The walks around campus that she refers to in the second post are ones in which she is on crutches but accompanied by friends. Janna also said that some nights she would walk the halls of the dorm floor she supervised as a resident assistant and doing so cleared her head more than remaining still and sedentary. October 18 is the first day she is cleared for exercise by her physical therapist, so she performs a "land workout" that re-energizes her creative process. One month later, at the end of her logging, she makes an uncharacteristic entry that reflects not only on that day but her logging journey overall. She does so in the form of a knowledge structure. To Janna, her physical rehabilitation becomes the process she can compare to her writing process. These processes are similar in that both require "steps that have to be taken to get where you want to be." By this final entry, we can see how much both of these processes mean to her as a generative thinker.

If there were ever any question as to whether or not Janna was truly capable of generative and restorative thinking, her written reflection on the logging exercise verifies that she is exceptionally capable of both. In the same way we witnessed some professional writers discuss how they shift between generative and restorative thinking fluidly, Janna can do the same. She writes,

Exercising and physically moving gives me the time that I need to think about the writing I need to get done during the day, as well as a moment to clear my mind after a busy schedule. I find myself thinking or creating stories in my mind that I could write in a future time, in addition to processing the written assignments I have for classes or the music that I needed to practice. Overall, I feel as though this writing log was of great help in forcing myself to slow down through the business of life in order to take time to care for myself physically and to understand both my writing process and myself even better than merely scraping the surface I was standing on. I was able to obtain more self-awareness and to deter from my typical binge writing ways as I have learned the importance of patterns, routine, and establishing writing boundaries for oneself in order to become not only a better writer, but a healthier one that deeply understands the self.

In the first two sentences, she establishes that she is able to shift between restorative thinking and generative thinking, saying that she uses her exercise time to clear her mind and to create stories. I wonder if she would have realized her latent embodied abilities had she not kept the log. Past conversations with Janna tell me that she may have, but I also believe the log helped her better understand the extent to which she is capable of both restorative and generative thinking by externalizing her reflections on a daily basis. The use of the word *force* is an interesting one that I hear from time to time in talking to writers about their logs. To think that a log applies force to make a writer slow down and contemplate their writing process is to imply that writers, however thoughtful they may be, rarely slow down to contemplate their embodied needs. Finally, in this excerpt we see that Janna believes logging made her more aware of unhealthy writing "patterns," including her propensity for binge writing. Binge writing, or writing for many hours without moving much or taking restorative mental breaks, can have deleterious effects on the writer's mind and make returning to writing more difficult in future sessions (Boice "Procrastination, Busyness, and Bingeing" 605). Without a doubt, the log provided some benefit to this productive young writer, particularly in terms of giving her more insight into healthy and unhealthy writing habits.

In more ways than one, I see Janna's case as being exceptional but informative for writers who think they want to approach embodied writing. First, Janna doubles as a student and a professional writer. The latter designation makes her case unusual because she has already developed advanced writerly habits that sustain her ability to craft longer works and to refine them for a public audience. At the same time, Janna is still a student writer, and at the time of her logging she was still in her earliest years of college. While there is much she knows intuitively through her committed practice, she is still learning new genres and techniques. Without delving into a lengthier discussion about how professional writers ought to remain students of their writing, Janna is a case to be included in the student section due to her newness in this field. Second, what is also interesting about Janna's case is that she experiences a disabling injury that challenged her ability to remain productive as a runner-writer. This injury and the surgery that followed derailed her triathlon training problems while making it difficult for her mind to "get around more." Her log entries and reflection document how her abilities as a writer suffered when she could not move her body as much or as well as she needed to in order to find comfort in her writing process. Regardless, she coped by finding other ways to move forward. She reported that even walking on crutches helped her enter a better mental headspace that enabled her to write. Therefore, whether a writer is a runner, a walker, or has been disabled by a recent injury, with some conscious effort that writer can still find ways to connect to their writing through embodied cognition.

CONCLUSION

In these student examples, we start to see very clearly how at first students do not always understand the benefits of embodied movement but that those benefits present real possibilities for knowledge-making and intellectual transformation. In many ways, we can begin to think of embodied writing as a deeper level of critical thinking or a higher level of creativity, one that is not easy for all students at all times. We also see that student writers have a difficult time wrapping their heads around the direct benefits of embodied movement on writing practices, but they benefited indirectly nonetheless. When we nudge our students to move and to write in embodied ways, we challenge them to grow as writers and to expand their repertoire of skills.

7 Finding the Finish: Recommendations for Writing with the Body

An involuntary toast of beer splatters across my cheek, into my mouth. I've been keeping pace with a woman in an emerald green tank top for the last three miles, but she just pulled ahead of me to snatch a can of lukewarm Pabst Blue Ribbon from her cheering section at mile twelve. The thought of consuming this runner's sweaty backwash makes me cringe, but the guttural hooping and hollering of her friends forces me to smile. We are so close.

I've been thinking about what I how I might write about this first half marathon. I keep coming back to ideas about the undoing of my former identity, the me that hated running and made fun of runners. The me in elementary school that was bookish, shy, and absolutely terrified of running the mile for the Presidential Physical Fitness Test for fear of side cramps and gasping for air like I was drowning. Running meant embarrassment and shame. Running used to make me feel less worthy of others' approval than those who could run the mile in under ten minutes.

The runner-writer I am now, in this moment, is managing to keep just under an eight-minute-mile pace while running so hard that the sole of my right shoe has ripped from heel to midsole and the dye of my fuchsia sports bra has visibly bled through my white technical shirt. The runner-writer I am now feels redeemed by the strength in my legs and the ideas for writing that are sending me forward.

Now I hear spectators clamoring with cowbells at the finish line, and I see the cerulean blue staging of the finish line up ahead. Runners who were flanking my sides for the last mile or so step on some secret button buried down deep in their shoes and are able to power past me now. I try to run faster, too, but my legs are almost numb from fatigue and my eyes grow wide at the spectacle of this final mile. I read people's names on signs, I watch what those ahead of me do once they cross over to the other side. They raise their arms, they high-five their friends, they take their finisher medals, and they pose for photos with a casual hand on one hip like it was all so easy.

I have no one waiting for me at this finish line. I still live alone in Ames. I broke up with my boyfriend of three years about a month ago, and I wasn't about to ask my grad school friends to drive down to Des Moines on a chilly fall morning to wait around for me.

But as I stumble around the crowds watching finishers hug their small children bundled up in layers to protect them from the first frost of fall, I'm seen by a friend of a friend, who calls me over. She congratulates me and tells me to take a picture with the sign she made for our mutual friend, Joe, a geneticist who is still running the half marathon somewhere. The sign reads "Motivational Sign. We are so proud of you, Joe." but she covers "Joe" with one hand as she poses with me. If you want to see benevolence in its sincerest form, stand at the finish line of a marathon or half marathon.

Katherine Switzer, the first woman to run the Boston Marathon, once said, "If you are losing faith in human nature, go out and watch a marathon." At a finish line, strangers cheer relentlessly for people they don't know. They shake signs and hand out water bottles. Sometimes they catch runners as they fall to a halting finish, carry an injured finisher to a medical care tent, or hug the running buddy they met along the way. We find ourselves at the finish line, humbled by the goodwill of others.

I have often asked myself what brings these kind-hearted onlookers out early on weekend mornings. Have they run a long-distance race, too? Did they have support through their training process? A cheer section waiting for them on the sidelines?

I turn the corner to search for post-race sustenance in the form of orange slices and school-sized chocolate milk cartons. I wonder what I'll tell my writing students on Monday when they ask if I made it to the end or not. I'm sure I can connect this finish line to the writing process.

INTRODUCTION

For years, I fumbled around databases trying to find other researchers who had studied running in connection to the writing process. Now, almost a decade later, I can much more confidently tell my writing students that any writer can hit their stride in terms of creativity and productivity when they tap into physical practices that support embodied writing processes. In the earliest chapters of this book, I have tried to empower writers to think about embodiment in the writing process from both a writing studies and an embodied cognition perspective. Running as a both a literal and literate physical practice that invites embodied cognition into the minds of runner-writers is one example of a physical activity that buttresses generative thinking, restorative thinking, and knowledge structuring. As I established in Chapter Six, running is not the only physical activity to be undertaken if writers want to tap into embodied cognition. For all writers, I will review key findings and discuss how to enact embodied writing for writers of all ability levels using three key phrases. For teachers of writing, I will share pedagogical recommendations for incorporating physical movement into the classroom and for supporting student writers with a range of bodily abilities, thinking especially in terms of being inclusive of all writers' bodily abilities and disabilities.

Key Findings

Across both groups of writers, professional and student, I have found that most writers related their physical activity to their writing activity in ways that align with embodied cognition research. Though the relationship between writing activity and physical activity is difficult to measure and sometimes especially difficult for student writers to grasp, novices and seasoned writers alike can benefit from tracking the interconnections between these two activities. My research confirms several key findings about the relationship between physical activity and writing activity:

- Most professional writers and student writers can engage in generative thinking, but professional writers are more likely to enact generative thinking than student writers.

- Most professional and student writers can engage in restorative thinking, but student writers are more inclined to describe restorative thinking than generative thinking experiences.

- As a physical practice, running is especially conducive to generative thinking when a writer can internally dissociate.

- Any physical practice can be used to awaken a writer's generative or restorative thinking capabilities with conscious control.

In the next section, I offer recommendations for writers and teachers of writing who want to launch into embodied writing but are not sure where to begin. Three memorable phrases can guide writers through the embodied writing process. Sequentially, these phrases prompt writers to get "Consciously in Command," to be "Leveraging Logging," and to be "Finding a Way Forward." Each phrase is explained within the framework of my theoretical concepts and rounded out with a "Try This" prompt to assist writers in their explorations of these phrases. For writing teachers in need of additional pedagogical recommendations, what follows "Finding a Way Forward" is additional advice on preparing to teach embodied writing that translates to any level of learning.

Recommendations

Consciously in Command

Conscious attention to the embodied writing practices of generative knowing, restorative knowing, or knowledge structuring require controlling the writer's mind while exercising. In my narrative introduction to Chapter Six, I shared how when I run I visualize my writer's brain as a dog on a leash. When my brain wants to veer off in another direction that is not my writing, I sometimes allow it to do so, but other times I pull myself back toward a centering thought, a title, a sentence, a word I want to lead with so that I regain control of my writing process while engaged in an act of embodiment. This process repeats over and over until I have hammered out the words I need to carry me forward with a particular project. Sometimes I stop to type those words into my phone or I hold tight to them until I have made my way back home to jot them down on a notepad. This process is messy and exploratory, but being in conscious control of our thinking means that we intentionally harness thoughts that serve our writing in a way that generates new ideas or consciously releases our mental grip on a writing project so that we can engage in restorative thinking.

Previously I discussed how writers who are also generative thinkers explain how they seize conscious control over their thoughts while running so that they focus on writing projects they need to think through before returning to their desk chairs. Several of my professional writer participants reported that the conscious or unconscious control of one's body and one's mind while engaging in physical activity has a sizable impact on the effectiveness of how they approach the writing process. The difference between conscious and unconscious control is a matter of the writer giving cognitive attention and focus to one's writing process while engaged in physical activity. As a qualitative researcher, I do not believe there is one instrument that can adequately assess a writer's unconscious or conscious control while exercising. I hold to be true the statements made by professional writers in Chapter Five that encourage us to ponder the concept of conscious control of one's physical activity in connection to one's writing activity. These statements make it easier to pinpoint when conscious control occurs. Imagine the writer who agonizes at a desk, racking the brain for creative insight, begging the muse to strike, and feeling like a failure only to create a perfectly good idea while doing something else—almost anything else you can imagine, like standing in the shower, pulling weeds in the garden, or brushing a dog's fur. These examples demonstrate unconscious control of embodied cognition, reaping the benefit of a new writing-related idea for having engaged in physical activity but not because one was aware of one's writing process or trying to create new writing ideas intentionally. Imagine the opposite scenario, in which the writer is intentional with their conscious control, thinking about ideas for writing while engaged in physical activity. When I think of conscious control as it relates to generative thinking, one of my favorite examples to visualize comes in a scene from *The Imitation Game*, when a camera lens close-up of emotionally straightforward codebreaker Alan Turing shows him sweating, pounding a gravel road while running away from the barn-like office where he has been writing solutions to break German codes during World War II. (The movie is based on Andrew Hodges's historical biography: *Alan Turing: The Enigma*, and the biography confirms that Turing was a seasoned marathoner.) It is while running that he gains new ideas for cracking the secret language Germans use to communicate war strikes, and this depiction most nearly defines embodied cognition.

My finding that professional writers are more likely to enact generative thinking than student writers should not detract from the inherent value of restorative thinking. Rest is an essential part of the writing process. I have defined restorative thinkers as writers who report restoring their cognitive functions while exercising, releasing the stress associated with writing to restore the mind for more writing activity later. Restorative thinkers make statements like these: "Running lets me zone out and get away from my writing" and "When I'm doing yoga, I let my brain stop thinking about writing projects and I find clarity." As we've discussed, rest is active and rest is a skill (Pang 11–15). Pang's theory of active rest shows that plenty of artists and other creative types engage in intensive exercise to stimulate restorative thinking. In a similar way, all writers benefit from restorative thinking, but knowing how to foster restorative thinking to the writer's benefit is, as Pang has claimed, a skill that few writers understand well enough to process consciously.

Conscious control will unfold and feel differently for every writer. My metaphor of the dog on the leash may help some writers but not all writers. This metaphor was introduced to me by a yoga teacher who uses it to help her meditate. Obviously, I have adapted this visualization to suit my needs as a writer. Other metaphors or visualizations might speak better to the lived experiences of other writers. For instance, if someone has never walked a dog, then my metaphor might preclude them from understanding how I consciously control my own generative thinking process. Each individual writer will have to fashion their own metaphor or visualization to suit their needs, and there are ways to track these developments. To work on being consciously in command of our writing while running and thinking, I describe in the next sections how and why writers should leverage logging to buttress their embodied writing habits and how all bodies may find a way forward with embodied writing through all means available to them.

Try this. Ask yourself: "What does my writing need right now?" If your answer to this question suggests you need to generate or work with existing content for a writing project, then decide what aspect of that project you want to think about as you move. If you need to mentally move away from your writing project, how can you ensure that the physical activity of your choice will enable you to do so?

Consider your conditions. Will the music or podcast you want to listen to distract you or give you new ideas? Will the weather conditions make thinking about writing feel easy for you? If not, can you adapt this activity to be performed indoors? Try to eliminate conditions that make engaging in generative or restorative thinking difficult.

Take notes if you are planning to generate content. Sentences are easily wordsmithed while in a creative state of motion and just as easily forgotten in the hours that follow. Some people prefer to stop exercising to type notes for writing in their iPhone and others prefer to scribble down ideas using pen and paper. Start to learn the most effective way for you to record these ideas so that you can make a habit of generative thinking.

Leveraging Logging

With a log in hand, any writer is better able to control for moments of generative or restorative thinking, and from there a writer can begin to determine their dominant preferences for generative or restorative thinking or even their ability to make knowledge structures. If not already familiar, a writing log is a mechanism for tracking a writer's progress toward a particular writing goal over a period of days, weeks, months, or years. Anyone who has committed to a NaNoWriMo (National Novel Writing Month) feat of writing 50,000 words or more in the month of November has probably logged into the organization's tracking platform to find a spreadsheet that shows trends in productivity. Likewise, people who track their daily step counts with fitness trackers or log exercises performed in apps, such as RunKeeper or MyFitnessPal, can easily generate reports for their own analysis so long as they remember to enter their data each day.

Logging daily running and writing activity supports regularity and accountability for many writers and runners by heightening awareness of embodied cognition and physical or creative progress made toward a writing goal. Despite a surprising lack of research on the usefulness of exercise and writing logs, a few studies confirm that the act of logging progress on a daily basis benefits the person who logs that information. For example, in 2010 exercise scientists Mark H. Anshel and Toto Sutarso published results from a study that followed the fitness regimens of forty-six university employees who had not engaged in physical exercise of any kind for at least thirty days or more prior to beginning the study. For ten weeks, the experimental group was coached to create written narrative reports of their exercise activities, and at the conclusion of the study only the experimental group gained a statistically significant increase in the rate of oxygen uptake during exercise and a decrease in body fat percentages (252). Writing about one's exercise experiences or progress appears to have a positive benefit, and the same seems to be true of logging writing. In one notable study by Robert Boice, twenty-seven academic writers were asked to write out their plans for writing during planned writing days at least five days a week for ten weeks. Boice published his results in *College Composition and Communication* in 1985, reporting that the nine writers in his experimental group produced eight times the average number of pages produced by his control group (writers who did not log writing ideas or commit to a regular writing practice) or his spontaneous group (those writers who logged ideas for writing when they randomly found time to write) (476).

Logging helps writers visualize clear connections between their physical activity and writing activity. In several of my studies I asked both professional and student writers to keep daily logs of their moving and writing practices. The logging templates provided were adaptable, and writers were encouraged to add columns or information in places that they thought would help them track their development from the start to the end of the logging period (See Appendix A). Across the board, I discovered that professional and student writers usually find the act of logging daunting, but those who successfully complete logs are better able to articulate the effects of generative or restorative thinking because they spent time carefully tracking their development and internal thoughts. Not only does logging improve one's regularity in terms of physical activity and writing activity, but logging also proved helpful in enabling writers to identify how their physical activity did or did not support their writing activity. More research is needed to determine how exactly writing logs should be designed to support student writers' exploration of embodied writing. Perhaps such logs will inspire student writers to adopt a habit that has proven useful for many professional writers, too.

Try This. Take inventory of any logging you currently do or have done in the past. What applications or formats have helped you stay disciplined and diligent? What has made logging helpful to you? What has made logging a hindrance at times? Determine your logging needs before choosing the correct logging instrument for you.

Research available logging applications or formats that might meet these needs. Will you use two separate applications for tracking physical activity and writing activity? If you prefer to track the two together, remember that you can look at the logging instrument used in my studies in Appendix A, and bear in mind that writers frequently adapt this log by adding columns for additional opportunities to reflect on their physical, emotional, and professional experiences or goals.

Choose a start date. Some people jump into logging right away only to find that they are met with professional, social, or familial demands that limit their ability to continue logging for some time, Once they stop they are less motivated to pick up their logs and start again. Although the chaos of life is unpredictable and uncontrollable, try to identify when you will begin logging and for how long you will log so that you are positioned to be successful. Successful logging begets successful writing practices; failed attempts at logging stymies progress, or worse, damages a writer's self-confidence.

Finding a Way Forward

Running is one form of physical activity that is conducive to both generating new knowledge for writing or restoring the mind for the work of writing, and it certainly is a good one. But running is not the only form of sensorimotor movement that benefits the writing process. If a writer seeks embodied writing, then she or he must find a way to move forward with a physical activity practice that is available. To understand what form is best for a writer, look inward to decide how to think best while moving.

When I recruited research participants, my intention was not to find writers who ran. In fact, I went out of my way to find writers interested in powerlifting, walking, yoga, soccer, and other individual and team-based physical activities. Much to my surprise, however, all of these participants shared a common interest in running. This coincidental finding is likely due to internal and external dissociation patterns of thinking, as described by Jeff Brown, in which some runners have the ability to cognitively focus their minds on internal thoughts (such as writing) and feelings as opposed to external observations or sensations. When writers like Brentney Hamilton internally dissociate while running, they are able to consciously think about their writing without having to stop, sit down, and write with a pen or a computer. Time spent thinking about writing is an act of prewriting that primes the writer to generate new knowledge for writing that benefits their writing practice later in the office, when they are not running.

Does this mean that, in comparison to other physical activities, running is more conducive to generative thinking? Perhaps, and if only because running involves repetitive motions that can become so rote and familiar that the runner can dedicate more mental space to other thoughts—writing prompts or problems, for example. On the contrary, elite marathoners are more likely to contend that running requires all of their cognitive attention and focus on external variables, such as weather conditions, speed, and pacing. One of my runner-writer participants, Joseph Darda, who finished first place in Fort Worth's 2020 Cowtown Marathon, cannot think about writing while running when he is trying to finish a 26.2-mile trek in less than two hours and thirty minutes. Inasmuch as running allows the mind some space to encounter our writing outside of our offices, we cannot generalize that every writer can and will prefer to write while running. We also cannot assume that every writer will feel safe and secure enough to spend their running or walking time thinking about their writing if visible parts of their intersectional identities—race, class, gender identity, sexual orientation, or religion—make running unsafe for them. Runners who face these dangerous realities might need to scan an area to see who is nearby or consider to how their bodies might be perceived by unfriendly onlookers. These safety concerns present a real barrier for anyone wanting to engage in embodied writing practice in public spaces. We must continue to think about how we can make moving in public spaces safer for all bodies.

An equally problematic and ableist generalization to make is that all bodies can run, or walk, or engage in any range of motion. When a student using a wheelchair enrolled in one of my courses in Spring 2018, I needed to rethink the walking meditation I described in Chapter Six. The Latin expression that guided my design of this activity, Solvitur Ambulando or "it is solved by walking," is a celebrated historical phrase that hardly seemed sensitive to the needs of my student who used a wheelchair. Worried that the language I had grown accustomed to in order to explain this concept would alienate this student, I decided the best way forward was to replace the word "walking" with "(st)rolling." My hope was that the student I had in the forefront of my mind would appreciate the visual subjugation of the two letters needed to turn the word rolling (a disability-focused word) into strolling (an ability-focused word). By diverting attention away from what able bodies can do and toward what all bodies could do in a more general movement sense, I hope that this student felt seen and appreciated for the embodied knowledge she could bring to this activity. Equally important is that I want to suggest to all students that embodied writing is available to all writers, not just those who are especially well conditioned or toned, and not those who boast impressive track records in running or other sports. The best way to engage with embodied writing is to find a way forward.

Finding a way forward will look different for every body. For some, embodied writing can be supported by running, but for many others embodied writing will be made possible while engaging on long walks, seated at a recumbent bike, zoning out in a group cycling class, or comfortably seated for a mindfulness meditation. Remember that as long as sensorimotor movement is involved—meaning attention is given to sensation and motor movements of any kind—embodied knowledge becomes attainable. For those suffering from chronic health conditions that incite pain and discomfort, finding a way forward will feel more arduous than for those who do not. For those who enjoy a certain level of physical fitness, it is important to be aware of how our bodies and our abilities change over time. The runner I was in 2012 is not the runner I am today. Patellofemoral pain syndrome, plantar fasciitis flare-ups, and two pregnancies have drastically altered my abilities (and not to mention humbled my ego) as a runner.

As a writing teacher, I invoke what I call (avail)able pedagogy, which is the belief that student writers retain autonomy over their bodies during the embodied writing process at all times. We must ensure that students are making all decisions about their writing bodies, and that the teacher is open to adapting embodied writing instruction and assessment to the needs of student bodies. Writing teachers must also recognize that students' corporeal needs may change over the course of several months or just a few minutes, and students are not likely to share such changes with teachers unless they feel comfortable discussing bodily differences with a trusting, supportive teacher. For this reason, I encourage embodied writing pedagogues to facilitate class discussions that explore issues of bodily difference and to cultivate in every classroom a community of student writers who honor bodily difference. These discussions should be held early and often so that students are reminded regularly of how a movement that is available to one peer may not be easily accessible to another peer. Only when student writers and their teachers foreground an embodied writing class with support for all ability levels of movement can we enact (avail)able pedagogy. In so doing, we assist our students and ourselves in finding new ways forward with movement in the writing process.

Making a physically safe, accessible entrance into different learning contexts also requires pedagogical finesse and attention to the available abilities students possess. If ableism is to blame for the physical and structural inequities defining academic centers of learning, then the antithesis—disablism or disability studies—is the obvious next embrace to be made by embodied writing pedagogues. Yet I am not convinced embodied writing pedagogy can rebrand so as to erase its ableist origins, nor can disability studies fully adopt embodied writing pedagogy without compromising the integrity of that field's collective mission. Because

I think both fields are interested one another, I want to offer the idea of an (avail)able pedagogy, which is how I define my current praxis. An (avail)able pedagogy does not revise instructional methods and materials in reaction to the presence of disability, but rather, tries as best as possible to anticipate the needs of students with disabilities while also encouraging contemplative, sensorimotor movement practices that enrich students' writing processes. Then, as new and unanticipated embodied needs arise, an (avail)able pedagogy responds sensitively and respectfully to those needs with appropriate accommodations.

Try This. Divide a sheet of paper into four quarters either by folding, drawing lines, or creating a table in a word processor. In the first quarter, write down every form of movement (avail)able to you that you can think of, and in the second quarter write down forms of movement that you physically cannot perform. Using the forms of (avail)able movement listed in the first quarter, choose which of those forms you enjoy most and list those in the third quarter. Finally, place in the fourth quarter forms of movement you do not enjoy and did not list in the third quarter.

Reflect on the forms of movement that were or were not (avail)able to you and those you enjoy most. Do you engage in the most (avail)able and enjoyable forms on a regular basis? Why or why not? What do you need to continue or rekindle your engagement with these forms of movement?

Ask your writing students to try this activity, which can be used as is or adapted to let students determine what is (avail)able and enjoyable to them as writers. Consider discussing with students what writing genres or skills feel (avail)able to them and which writing genres or skills present obstacles to their learning process. Also, take time to discuss with student writers what writing genres or skills they most enjoy to better understand their abilities as well as the obstacles they face as writers.

Pedagogical Recommendations

We can teach students to engage in both generative and restorative thinking if we embrace an (avail)able pedagogy that responds to the embodied needs of all learners. Embodied thinking can occur organically, as many of the professional writers featured in this book have discovered, but how might we approach the teaching embodied writing with more intentionality, more interest in fostering students' physical abilities and disabilities in connection to their writing processes? For writing teachers interested in this new pedagogical terrain, I can offer a few recommendations for successfully incorporating sensorimotor movement into a writing course.

Before I do, though, it is critical to understand that preparing for students to move their bodies in classrooms requires a thoughtful approach to production. This reality is due in large part to the fact that the standard writing classroom is not designed for physical movement. Most university classrooms are built economically—meaning these classrooms tend to be modest in size—and are designed for sitting with many desks and chairs squeezed into an already tight enclosure. Except for the small well of space that the instructor uses to move about while leading class discussions, little other open space is available to instructors and students. Plus, with the invitation to move comes the invitation to make mistakes: to fall, to lose balance, or to decrease the amount of personal space that exists between bodies. Considering all of these constraints, in the following sections I will discuss the importance of setting up, continuing one's education, exploring instructor and student movement histories, seeking administrative support, and carrying out instruction effectively.

Setting Up

Arranging one's writing classroom in advance of instruction is key. Anyone who has ever tried to remove all the tables and chairs from a classroom knows that moving these pieces of furniture is no simple task. Moving seating for twenty can take a significant portion of class time, especially if no time is available before the start of class to begin the process of moving furniture out into the hall or another classroom. If an alternative classroom space is accessible to your students, then switching to another location is a better solution. The first time I taught Yoga-Zen Writing, I was able to secure a large studio space in TCU's recreation center, which provided my students plenty of room to spread out, dimmed lighting, and yoga mats at no extra cost. In the second semester I taught Yoga-Zen Writing at TCU, the recreation center staff informed me of a new policy that required all studio space users to pay a seventy-five-dollar fee. Being financially compromised as a graduate student instructor at the time, I located and reserved other traditional classrooms on campus that were larger than our own. Of course, every university's classroom scheduling system is different. Regardless of size and availability, all instructors ought to assess the space available to students well in advance of the time when students begin to move. If an instructor will have students practicing yoga, bringing a standard-sized yoga mat (twenty-four inches wide by sixty-eight inches long) to the classroom can help you measure out roughly how many mats can fit into a classroom space. Knowing how and where students' mats will fit in your classroom will also help you plan where you will be stationed during the session.

If you plan to lead students in an embodied exercise outside, the two biggest considerations are weather and audiovisual accessibility for all students. Inclement weather or soggy turf can put a damper on plans for embodied writing, and the lack of audiovisual equipment may preclude students with vision or hearing impairments. For these reasons, I plan embodied writing activities to be adaptable to learners seated at a desk or standing in front of their desks, taking special care to ensure that all movements are accessible. My experiences in teaching yoga have trained me to say to students at the start of an embodied movement session that "Anyone can modify any of these movements at any time. Do not feel as though you need to do what others are doing. Do what your body needs." If I worry about an exercise making students feel self-conscious or if the exercise would just as easily be conducted at home, then I provide thorough written instructions so that the exercise can be completed as homework.

Continuing Education

Writing instructors should invest time in the study and practice of a physical activity before teaching or sharing that activity in the writing classroom. I began teaching Yoga-Zen Writing with about eight years of experience as a yoga practitioner. During the second semester I taught this course, I was nearly finished with my 200-Hour Registered Yoga Teacher Certification from the Yoga Alliance. Engaging in these continuing education activities were the best possible means for teaching and learning more about yoga with my students. Of course, a 200-hour teacher training course requires significant commitment, dedication, and money to complete, but I pursued this training because I wanted to understand the poses in greater depth than I did when I had no formal training in yoga instruction. I wanted to plan more meaningful movement sequences, to improve my ability to assist students in movement and relaxation techniques, and to study the differences and similarities between teaching the body and teaching the mind. I do not think a professional certification is necessary to introduce movement into the classroom. In fact, instructors can integrate online, pre-packaged resources, such as meditation recordings or Christy Wenger's "Yoga Asana Handout." However, my study and practice of yoga taught me critical lessons I would not have otherwise known had I not continued my education. I would not have known that veterans, domestic abuse survivors, or other victims of trauma may not feel comfortable closing their eyes during meditation due to the effects of post-traumatic stress disorder. I am sure I would have overlooked the fact that non-traditional students may have a limited range of motion available to them. The human body is a richly complicated structure that can be overwhelming to understand to un-trained professionals, but that is why embodied writing research matters. For too long the effects of the human body on writing processes have been ignored, and only through careful study and understanding of the body can we begin to recognize how writers create new knowledge with and through their bodies.

Administrative Support

Instructors should discuss their plans to introduce physical movement to students with their campus disability services office and with their writing program administrator (WPA). If a student were to encounter an issue with a movement or have an unforeseen accommodation—such as a physical limitation, handicap, or injury—strategizing alternative learn-ing opportunities with disability services is in the best interest of the stu-dent and, potentially, other students with invisible disabilities that they are hesitant to reveal. In a best-case scenario, a disability services office and a WPA are provided ample time to look over proposed instructional materials to provide feedback on scenarios that might prove troublesome or hazardous.

Student Resistance

Student resistance is a natural reaction to embodied writing processes because students, like instructors, are entering into unfamiliar pedagogi-cal territory. As discussed in the previous chapter, even the most open-minded of my students reported feelings of internal resistance when prompted to move and write about how movement affected their writing processes. In the case of LeAnna, we saw how one student could re-flect on her walking meditation experience as a struggle from the outset because walking and thinking about writing felt like an arduous task. Nevertheless, the written reflection LeAnna submitted was shaped by a creative metaphor, a kind of knowledge structure she learned about her writing process as a result of generating thoughts for writing while walking. Student writers sometimes face internal resistance to generative thinking because traditional classroom structures deter embodied movement within the learning environment. Even so, I have found that the writing processes of student writers, like professional writers, are rewarded by diligent commitment to embodied cognition strategies that will enhance their productivity or creativity.

Emotion and Embodiment

Finally, emotion is a central part of embodied writing—albeit often overlooked—as already seen in the statements made by professional writing participant Thomas Gardner and student writing participants Vanessa and LeAnna. I would be remiss if I did not touch on the delicate nature of the emotional-embodied subject position of students in the writing classroom. This research focuses more on the embodied subject position of the student writer, recognizing that embodied writing has the ability to empower student writers, especially women who are aware of and willing to reflect on certain embodied-emotional issues. Although as embodied movement can be physically and emotionally empowering to students, I would recommend that all teachers be prepared for students to emote in ways that challenge but oftentimes strengthen their identities while also challenging our sense of professional objectivity as writing teachers. If a teacher feels professionally uncomfortable supporting such writing, then inviting embodied movement into the classroom is not advisable. As I stated in Chapter Six, it is far more difficult to teach a body than a mind, in my opinion, as someone who was a writing teacher first, a yoga teacher later. For any teacher willing to design a course around embodied writing, there are powerful embodied cognition effects to be felt by both teacher and student, but teachers must be prepared to address and support the emotions ensnared in these effects.

CONCLUSION

Perhaps the greatest contradiction of embodied writing is that it is a natural process that feels unnatural. We all write from bodies, bodies that experience aches and pains, bursts of energy and afternoon slumps, a need to move and a need to be intensely still. Whether or not we realize it, we are all engaged in embodied writing because we write from our own embodied subject positions all the time. Our bodies influence what we write and how we write it.

As we have seen in the portraits and profiles of writers featured in this book, most of us write without giving much thought to what our bodies are doing while we write. Or if we have developed a method for connecting our bodies to our writing processes, we keep this discovery to ourselves. Some professional writers, such as Joyce Carol Oates, Haruki Murakami, George Sheehan, Christie Wright Wild, and Thomas Gardner, have professed the virtues of embodied writing with others as if they were sharing a best kept secret of the trade. Nevertheless, contemporary writing curricula does not make space for instruction on body-based writing practices. The handful of student writers included in this book have all benefited from inviting sensorimotor movement and meditation into their writing processes in highly individualized ways, speaking loudly to the untapped potential of this area of pedagogical research.

All of the writers I have interviewed and studied build an intriguing corpus of narratives from which we can begin to understand the embodied writing we do intentionally and that which we do unintentionally every day. On some level, all writers intuitively know how to run, think, and write because all writers know how to see relationships connecting their movement patterns to their thinking and writing patterns. For these reasons and more, I hope that the field of embodied writing continues to expand forward into composition's future. There has never been a better time to run a little longer and a little farther with our writing.

Notes

1. The deck is a line of text that typically comes after the title and before the author's byline.

2. After consulting with Richard Leo Enos, I took it upon myself to locate this famous quotation. Neither the *Phaedrus* nor the *Republic* include it. In other academic articles, it is attributed to several quotation repository websites (see Mull and Tietjen-Smith 1). Although exact attribution cannot be provided, its widespread popularity and use render it useful and worthwhile to this discussion.

3. Much later, when Roman educators would adopt and then adapt much of Greek curriculum, athletics would be left behind, along with other content areas deemed "electives" by today's standards (Rifenburg 9).

4. The parameters of this project did not position me to study writers who identify as having non-normative bodies. This coupled with the fact that my project assumes all bodies are capable of embodied cognition through various forms of sensorimotor movement—from the slightest tapping of keyboard keys to the seemingly sedentary act of meditating—moved attention away from the study of non-normative bodies in a hyper-focused sense. In my conclusion, I will discuss implications for disability studies and non-normative bodies in embodied cognition research.

5. For another relevant study on student-athletes that focuses more on learning to write by means of learning play calls and play embodiment, see J. Michael Rifenburg's *The Embodied Playbook*.

6. Note that Perl's concept of felt sense appears to be rooted in I. A. Richards's four kinds of meaning, which includes sense, feeling, tone, and intention. Sense refers to the meaning the writer is making with words, quite literally, and how she or he is referring to them.

7. Of note is the fact that many literary writers were avid walkers, especially Romantic poets, such as William Wordsworth.

8. Zazen is synonymous with Zen or Zen Buddhism, which adopts a practice of sitting and suspending all judgmental thoughts to achieve greater inner peace and insight.

9. The mind-body connection is a misleading distinction in that the mind is never completely apart from the body in any area of the body or in any bodily process. Consider the nerve endings on your fingers. These nerves are part of the larger nervous system and are constantly taking in messages from inside and outside the body to alert the brain to feelings of touch. If one were to press into the ground with one's fingers while the body is engaged in a yoga pose, one is sending messages to the brain that generate cognitive activity, which in turn may open the door for embodied cognition to take place.

10. Of all these claims and some of the examples Wilson provides, she never comments on how these claims could apply to writing. Any comparisons being made between writing and running are my own for reader application.

11. I choose not to differentiate between jogging and running. Most assume jogging is the slower version of running. Some contend that jogging requires a radically different physical form and so the two are separate. Jogging as a term was popularized when recreational running took hold of American culture in the 1960s, and the preferred term became running in the following decade (McKenzie 7). For clarity's sake, I will use the term running throughout.

12. Often cited for their propensity for walking on foot are the peripatetic philosophers. Etymologically, the word peripatetic is derived from root words meaning "walking" and "around."

13. O'Mara discusses how running is an equally if not more powerful activity for increasing BDNF production than walking, but running comes with a higher risk of injury over time (140).

14. It was through conversations with other writers that I was encouraged to think about physical activity in expansive terms. In participant interviews, discerning between running and walking, for example, invited more confusion than I expected. For instance, I was asked clarification questions about how fast or at what pace one must run to be considered running? Does a run still count if you are required to take a walking break? Does a circuit of running in a CrossFit program count as running, or what if someone has ideas for writing throughout all three legs of a triathlon—swimming, biking, and running? With these questions in mind, I developed questions that invited curiosity about physical

activity in a universally inclusive way, and the answers I found took me in a more specific direction toward walking and running.

15. The collection of qualitative interview data allowed for maximal flexibility in gathering data that differed from participant-to-participant, honoring individual differences as examples for improving our understanding of the relationship between physical activity and writing activity. For information on my grounded theory approach to coding, please see Appendix B.

16. These two conceptual states of thinking were not the first terms I tried on. When I first began coding my data, I titled these writers as either endurance writers or incremental writers. In that division, a lucid difference arose. Some writers articulated their tendency to exercise for two or more hours once a week in connection to their tendency to write for two hours or more a day, while for others, exercising or writing for long periods of time was a challenge due to professional obligations. Therefore, this division did not capture the extremes to which some of my participants go to in terms of their physical exercise regimens, nor did it accurately reflect those waning in intensity with their physical fitness at times. I also attempted to use the term pairing of generative writers and restorative writers as well as Boice's pair of terms: "discipline thinkers" versus "free thinkers." Ultimately, the terms generative thinking and restorative thinking proved to be the most all-encompassing terms for this research, especially since those terms reflect composition scholar Ann E. Berthoff's use of the term thinking.

17. At the end of this section, I take pause to assure the reader that the knowledge structures these writers reveal were not unduly influenced in that the questions on physical activity and writing activity were separated and made to be distinct from one another. As any of the recordings will demonstrate, the participants were never prompted to connect the two activities studied in this project. Any connections writers made to past physical experiences were not prompted by me because I discovered and developed the concept of knowledge structuring after analyzing the interview transcripts, not before.

18. Women who exercise in pregnancy give birth to babies who boast lower resting heart rates and greater heart-rate variability, which indicates good health for the cardiac and nervous systems of infants (May 213). Additionally, exercise has a positive effect on infant birth weight, shown to reduce the risk of Type 2 Diabetes quite substantially (Whincup et al. 2886).

19. Every participant was offered the opportunity to choose their own pseudonym by writing in a preferred name in order to remain anonymous. I gather from multiple conversations with participants that anonymity was not desirable because the participant was already a very public figure in their role as a writer or academic writer. Nevertheless, participants were reminded that they may follow up with me at any time if they changed their minds regarding their participation in this study or if they would prefer to remain anonymous.

20. Every writer in this study reported strong preferences for running outside, which was not surprising given the research available on outdoor exercise, referred to in some fields as green exercise. Studies have shown that green exercise leads to improved health benefits, "improve[d] mood and self-esteem," and "meditative effect[s] [that] distract from the monotony of the experience" (Hitchings and Latham 505).

21. See Appendix C for a list of the interview questions used in my study. Some of these questions were developed based on Boice's discussion of practice as opposed to performance in writing in *How Writers Journey to Comfort and Fluency.* I also borrow Boice's terms, *motivation, imagination,* and *control,* which were found to be critical aspects of writing performance for careerist writers in academic and nonacademic work.

22. For this project, I contemplated creating a third state of writing to describe writers who consistently moved between states of generative and restorative thinking on a frequent basis. However, my data shows that the majority of writers studied could move between generative and restorative thinking rather quickly, some with exceptional ease. Therefore, I chose not to devise a third state of thinking, but to focus instead on the differences between these two states and how writers distinguish between these two states.

23. My division of the effects of thinking into two separate terms is not intended to suggest that these ways of thinking are exclusive or independent of each other. Rather, this division naturally presented itself while coding the participants' interview data.

24. All writers were asked if they had relevant writing samples to share with me for further analysis. Some writers willingly shared samples that they deemed relevant to our discussion. In the case of one writer, for example, his thoughts on the relationship between writing and running were available for reading online and in book form. In the case of the second poet, however, he explained that he had no samples of writing that spoke to his physical activities in a way that might connect to his writing

activities. In cases of the latter, I chose not to press writers for samples they did not willingly share or volunteer. Instead, I chose to trust the judgment of my participants and maintain their good favor as a writing researcher.

25. To be clear, knowledge structuring is not a term that Wild coined. Rather, I created this term to describe the way she and other writers apply physical activity terms to writing activity scenarios.

26. In Chapter Three, I introduced Jeff Brown's sports psychology framework for understanding when and how the mind zones out. The practice of dissociation occurs when runners takes their mind off the act of running and focus instead on non-running concerns, such as personal relationships or work projects.

27. To protect the identities of student writers, all participants were given the option to choose their own pseudonyms, have a pseudonym chosen for them, or go by their first name.

28. This course is typically taken by first-year students at TCU as a general education requirement, and the class met twice a week for eighty minutes per class period.

29. Two students enrolled in this course successfully had their work published—one in a local newspaper and the other on a mental health and well-being site.

30. See Appendix B for more information on grounded theory research.

31. At TWU, the next greatest percentage of minority students is African-American (18.2%) followed by Asian students (10%), international students (1.6%), Native American students (1.2%), students identifying as Other (.6%), and Pacific-Islander students (.4%) ("TWU Institutional Research").

32. It does not appear as though ethnicity had any bearing on students' ability to engage with generative or restorative thinking, but it is possible that it may have since I did not directly ask students to speak to these aspects of their identities as writers. In the future, I hope to take a closer look at how embodied writing unfolds differently in different cultural contexts and discourse communities outside of the academic classroom.

Works Cited

Aitchison, Callum, et al. "Inner Dialogue and Its Relationship to Perceived Exertion During Different Running Intensities." *Perceptual and Motor Skills*, vol. 117, no. 1, 2013, pp. 1053–72.

Anderson, Monica. "The Hashtag #BlackLivesMatter Emerges: Social Activism on Twitter." *The Pew Research Center*, 15 Aug. 2016. https://www.pewresearch.org/internet/2016/08/15/the-hashtag-blacklivesmatter-emerges-social-activism-on-twitter/

Anshel, M. H., and T. Sutarso. "Effect of A Storyboarding Technique on Selected Measures of Fitness among University Employees." *Research Quarterly for Exercise and Sport*, vol. 81, no. 3, 2010, pp. 252–63.

Bazerman, Charles, and Howard Tinberg. "Writing Is an Expression of Embodied Cognition." *Naming What We Know: Threshold Concepts of Writing Studies*, edited by Linda Adler-Kassner and Elizabeth Wardle, UP of Colorado, 2015.

Berman, Marc G., et al. "The Cognitive Benefits of Interacting with Nature." *Psychological Science*, vol. 19, no. 12, 2008, pp. 1207–12.

Berthoff, Ann E. *Forming, Thinking, Writing*. 2nd ed., Boynton/ Cook Publishers, 1988.

—. *Reclaiming the Imagination: Philosophical Perspectives for Writers and Teachers of Writing*. Boynton/ Cook Publishers, 1984.

—. *The Sense of Learning*. Heinemann, 1990.

Blakeslee, Ann, and Cathy Fleischer. *Becoming a Writing Researcher*. Routledge, 2010.

Boice, Robert. *Advice for New Faculty Members: Nihil Nimus*. Allyn and Bacon, 2000.

—. *How Writers Journey to Comfort and Fluency: A Psychological Adventure*. Praeger, 1994.

—. *Procrastination and Blocking: A Novel, Practical Approach*. Praeger, 1996.

—. "Procrastination, Busyness, and Bingeing." *Behaviour Research and Therapy*, vol. 27, no. 6, 1989, pp. 605–11.

—. *Professors as Writers: A Self-Help Guide to Productive Writing*. New Forums P, 1990.

—. "The Neglected Third Factor in Writing: Productivity." *College Composition and Communication*, vol. 36, no. 4, 1985, pp. 472–80.

Brown, Jeff. *The Runner's Brain*. Rodale, 2015.

Cavell, Stanley. *The Senses of Walden: An Expanded Edition*. U of Chicago P, 1981.

Cheville, Julie. *Minding the Body: What Student Athletes Know about Learning*. Boynton/ Cook, 2001.

Connolly, Cathleen T., and Christopher M. Janelle. "Attentional Strategies in Rowing: Performance, Perceived Exertion, and Gender Considerations." *Journal of Applied Sport Psychology*, vol. 15, 2003, p. 195–212.

Connolly, Cathleen T., and Gershon Tenenbaum. "Exertion-Attention-Flow Linkage Under Different Workloads." *Journal of Applied Social Psychology*, vol. 40, no. 5, 2010, pp. 1123–45.

Dutch, Taylor. "Running Needs Something More Radical Than Body Positivity. Here's How Latoya Shauntay Snell Is Making It Happen." *Runner's World*, 22 Oct. 2020.

Erickson, Kirk I., et al. "Exercise Training Increases Size of Hippocampus and Improves Memory." *Proceedings of the National Academy of Sciences of the United States*, vol. 108, no. 7, 2011, pp. 3017–22.

Farkas. Kerrie R. H., and Christina Haas. "A Grounded Theory Approach for Studying Writing and Literacy." *Practicing Research in Writing Studies: Reflexive and Ethnically Responsible Research*, edited by Katrina M. Powell and Pamela Takayoshi. Hampton P, 2012, pp. 81–96.

Faulkner, Sandra. *Real Women Run: Running as Feminist Embodiment*, Routledge, 2018.

Fleckenstein, Kristie S. "Writing Bodies: Somatic Mind in Composition Studies." *College English*, vol. 61, no. 3, Winter 1999, pp. 281–306.

Goddard, Tara, et al. "Racial Bias in Driver Yielding Behavior at Crosswalks." *Transportation Research Part F: Traffic Psychology and Behaviour*, vol. 33, 2015, pp. 1–6.

Hallett, M., and J. Grafman. "Executive Function and Motor Skill Learning." *International Review of Neurobiology*, vol. 41, 1997, pp. 297–323.

Hawhee, Debra. *Bodily Arts: Rhetoric and Athletics in Ancient Greece*. U Texas P, 2004.

Hitchings, Russell and Alan Latham. "Indoor Versus Outdoor Running: Understanding How Recreational Exercise Comes to Inhabit Environments through Practitioner Talk." *Transactions*, vol. 41, no. 4, 2016, 503–14.

Isocrates. *Isocrates I*. Translated by David C. Mirhady and Too Lee Yun, U of Texas P, 2000.

Jabr, Ferris. "Why Walking Helps Us Think." *The New Yorker*, 3 Sept. 2014. https://www.newyorker.com/tech/annals-of-technology/walking-helps-us-think

Jennings, Jay. "Why Is Running So White?" *Runner's World*, 15 Nov. 2011.

Kennedy, Tammie M., et al. *Rhetorics of Whiteness: Postracial Hauntings in Popular Culture, Social Media, and Education*. Southern Illinois UP, 2016.

Knoblauch, A. Abby. "Bodies of Knowledge: Definitions, Delineations, and Implications of Embodied Writing in the Academy." *Composition Studies*, vol. 40, no. 2, 2012, pp. 50–65.

Kuo, CY. "Sensorimotor-Conceptual Integration in Free Walking Enhances Divergent Thinking for Younger and Older Adults." *Frontiers in Psychology*, vol. 7, Fall 2016, p. 1580.

LeMesurier, Jennifer Lin. "Mobile Bodies: Triggering Bodily Uptake through Movement." *College Composition and Communication*, vol. 68 no. 2, 2016, pp. 292–316.

MacNealy, Mary Sue. *Strategies for Empirical Research in Writing*. Allyn and Bacon, 1999.

Mancuso, Carolina. "Bodies in the Classroom: Integrating Physical Literacy," *The Journal of the Assembly for Expanded Perspectives on Learning*, vol. 12, no. 1, 2006, pp. 25–35.

May, E. et al. "Aerobic Exercise during Pregnancy Influences Fetal Cardiac Autonomic Control of Heart Rate and Heart Rate Variability." *Early Human Development*, vol. 86, no. 4, 2010, 213–17.

McClelland, Elizabeth, Anna Pitt, and John Stein. "Enhanced Academic Performance Using a Novel Classroom Physical Activity Intervention to Increase Awareness, Attention and Self-Control: Putting Embodied Cognition into Practice." *Improving Schools*, vol. 18, no. 1, 2015, pp. 83–100.

Micciche, Laura. *Doing Emotion: Rhetoric, Writing, Teaching*. Boynton/Cook, 2007.

McKenzie, Shelly. *Getting Physical: The Rise of Fitness in American Culture*. U of Kansas P, 2013.

Montessori, Maria, and Barbara Carter. *The Secret of Childhood*. Orient Longmans, 1936.

Morgan, W. P., and M. L. Pollock, R. H. Maki. "Psychologic Characterization of The Elite Distance Runner." *Annals of the New York Academy of Sciences*, vol. 301, no. 1, 382–403.

Mull, Haley, and Tara Tietjen-Smith. "Physical Activity and Academic Success: Links on a University Campus." *Focus on Colleges, Universities, and Schools*, vol. 8, no. 1, 2014, pp. 1–8.

Nagamatu, L. S. et al. "Physical Activity Improves Verbal and Spatial Memory in Older Adults with Probable Mild Cognitive Impairment: A 6-Month Randomized Controlled Trial." *Journal of Aging Research*, vol. 2013, no. 1, 2013, pp. 1–10.

Oaten, M., and K. Cheng. "Longitudinal Gains in Self-Regulation from Regular Physical Exercise." *British Journal of Health Psychology*, vol. 11, no. 4, Fall 2006, pp. 717–33.

O'Mara, Shane. *In Praise of Walking: The New Science of How We Walk and Why It's Good for Us*. Penguin Random House, 2019.

Ong, Walter J. *Orality and Literacy: The Technologizing of the Word.* Routledge, 1982.

Oppezzo, M., and D. L. Schwartz. "Give Your Ideas Some Legs: The Positive Effect of Walking on Creative Thinking." *Journal of Experimental Psychology,* vol. 40, no. 4, Summer 2014, pp. 1142–52.

Osgood-Campbell, Elisabeth. "Investigating the Educational Implications of Embodied Cognition: A Model Interdisciplinary Inquiry in Mind, Brain, and Education Curricula." *Mind, Brain and Education,* vol. 9, no. 1, 2015, pp. 3–9.

Perl, Sondra. *Felt Sense: Writing with the Body.* Heinemann, 2004.

—. "Understanding Composing." *College Composition and Communication,* vol. 31, no. 4, Winter 1980, pp. 363–369.

Petrzela, Natalia Mehlman. "Jogging Has Always Excluded Black People." *The New York Times,* 12 May 2020.

Richards, I. A. *Practical Criticism: A Study of Literary Judgment.* Harvest Books, 1956.

Rifenburg, J. Michael. *The Embodied Playbook: Writing Practices of Student Athletes.* Logan, Utah State UP, 2018.

Ripatrazone, Nick. "Why Writers Run." *The Atlantic Online,* 11 Nov. 2015.

Running USA. "Running USA's 2020 Global Runner Survey - North American Edition." Nov. 2020.

Schulz, Kathryn. "What We Think about When We Run." *New Yorker Online,* 3 Nov. 2015.

Segal, S. K. et al. "Exercise-Induced Noradrenergic Activation Enhances Memory Consolidation in Both Normal Aging and Patients with Amnestic Mild Cognitive Impairment." *Journal of Alzheimer's Disease,* vol. 32, no. 4, 2012, pp. 1011–18.

Selzer, Jack, and Sharon Crowley. *Rhetorical Bodies.* U of Wisconsin P, 1999.

Sheehan, George. *Running and Being: The Total Experience.* Rodale, 2013.

TCU Office of Institutional Research. *2015 Fact Book: Interactive Fact Book Navigation,* 2015.

Thompson, Becky. "Teaching with Tenderness: Toward an Embodied Practice." U of Illinois P. 2017.

Tine, Michelle T., and Allison G. Butler. "Acute Aerobic Exercise Impacts Selective Attention: An Exceptional Boost in Lower-Income Children." *Education Psychology,* vol. 32, no. 7, 2012, pp. 821–34.

TWU Office of Institutional Research and Data Management. *TWU Fact Book,* 2019.

Varela, Francisco J., Evan Thompson, and Eleanor Rosch. *The Embodied Mind: Cognitive Science and Human Experience.* The MIT P, 1993.

Voss, M.I. et al. "Plasticity of Brain Networks in a Randomized Intervention Trial of Exercise Training in Older Adults." *Aging Neuroscience,* vol. 20, no. 2, 2010, pp. 1–17.

Weber, Max. "Wissenschaft als Beruf." *Gesammlte Ausfsaetze zur Wissenschaftslehre.* Translated by H. H. Gerth and C. Wright Mills. Oxford UP, 1946.

Weinberg, R. S. et al. "Effect of Association, Dissociation and Positive Self-Talk Strategies on Endurance Performance." *Canadian Journal of Applied Sport Sciences*, vol. 9, no. 1, 1984, pp. 25–32.

Wenger, Christy I. Personal interview. 5 July 2016.

—. "Writing Yogis: Breathing Our Way to Mindfulness and Balance in Embodied Writing Pedagogy." *The Journal of the Assembly for Expanded Perspectives on Learning*, vol. 18, no. 1, 2012, pp. 24–39.

—. *Yoga Minds, Writing Bodies: Contemplative Writing Pedagogy.* The WAC Clearinghouse/Parlor P, 2015.

"What Runners Want You to Know about Being LGBTQ+ in Our Sport." *Runner's World*, 30, Oct. 2020.

Wilson, Margaret. "Six Views of Embodied Cognition." *Psychonomic Bulletin and Review*, vol. 9, no. 4, 2002, pp. 625–36.

Whincup, P. H. et al., "Birthweight and Risk of Type 2 Diabetes: A Systematic Review." *Journal of the American Medical Association*, vol. 300, no. 24, December 24, 2008, pp. 2886–97.

Yagelski, Robert. *Writing as a Way of Being: Writing Instruction, Nonduality, and the Crisis of Sustainability.* Hampton P, 2011.

Appendix A

YOUR WEEKLY WRITING-MOVING LOG

Use the table to describe the daily/ weekly writing goals you set at the start of each week. Feel free to explain how the log will be marked to track your goals however you like (e.g., minutes spent writing, pages written, texts produced, etc.). An example log that I filled out to share with participants follows.

Day/ Date	Pre-Writing Goal	Post-Writing Assessment of Goal	Daily Physical Activity Goal	Reflections/ Comments
Monday				
Tuesday				
Wednesday				
Thursday				
Friday				
Saturday				
Sunday				

SAMPLE LOG

Day/ Date	Pre-Writing Goal	Post-Writing Assessment of Goal	Daily Physical Activity Goal	Reflections/ Comments
Monday	Write 500 words for *DMN*	Goal achieved, but need to edit	Cycle, 40 minutes	It's harder for me to write and work out on Mondays.
Tuesday	Attend writing group, write for an hour in evening	Attended discussion, chose to edit yesterday's piece	Yoga Class, 60 minutes	I think yoga makes me anxious to write more because it's not as fast paced as running or cycling.
Wednesday	Submit piece to DMN, write IRB Documents	Goals achieved!	Run, 50 minutes or 5 miles	I LOVE longer mornings for running that always seem to coincide with my longer days for writing.
Thursday	No writing time today	None.	Strength training, 40 minutes	I feel guilty for not having time to write today, but I did really need to cross-train with strength to keep all my muscles firing properly. Maintenance woes, I guess.
Friday	Write for 2 hours at group writing time	Goal achieved!	HIIT training, 40 minutes	Just glad to have hit another goal!
Saturday	Finalize dissertation chapter 1 edits	Made progress but must finish tomorrow	Cycle, 60 minutes	I love having long Saturday mornings for writing & cycling, but sitting so long after working out make me a little crabby.
Sunday	Finalizing dissertation chapter edits	Finished, goal achieved!	Rest Day	I kind of hate rest days but I definitely needed the time to round out all my thoughts on this chapter.

Appendix B

To study writing as an embodied activity requires recognition that bodies differ, and at the same time, differing bodies may share common mental and physical experiences. Qualitative interviews, then, were the best means for uncovering a range and variety of quality data to understand this relationship. The collection of qualitative interview data allowed for maximal flexibility in gathering data that differed from participant-to-participant, honoring individual differences as examples for improving our understanding of the relationship between physical activity and writing activity. As noted in the section on data collection, methods other than interviewing were used, such as analysis of shared or publicly available texts composed by participants, but interviews were the primary data collected. With these data sets to be collected, my process was guided by a grounded theory approach to analysis.

Because the nature of the relationship between writing activity and physical activity is not well understood by compositionists, my approach to data analysis was informed by the principles of grounded theory. In this methodology, data collected in a relatively new, interdisciplinary, or under-researched area of study are read and coded in order to identify themes that emerge. According to Kerrie R. H. Farkas and Christina Haas, grounded theory is often called "the constant comparison method" that is best understood as "a set of explicit, iterative strategies primarily based on the act of comparison" (82). Where there is not an existing theory to describe a relationship, like the relationship that seems to exist between writing activity and physical activity, grounded theory prepares researchers to look at data while simultaneously constructing new theoretical frameworks. For my research, using determined coding themes featured in other studies influencing my project, such as the ones designed by Boice, would have been insensitive and would not have captured the curious nature of this relationship for student writers in particular. Moreover, Boice's terms were developed to capture the strategies of academic writers who are mostly sedentary, neither professional writers nor deeply embodied writers in academia or in other writing fields.

CODING BY CONSTANT COMPARISON PROCESS

In keeping with a grounded theory approach, my data coding by constant comparison commenced when my interviews began. The first stage in my coding process was to note possible themes for analysis as I listened to participants share their narratives during the interview process. These pen-and-paper notes became time markers as well as reminders to revisit and reflect on what a participant had said at a certain point in the interview that resonated with comments made by other participants or comments that were markedly different from what previous participants had said. Before determining what themes I would code for, I transcribed most every word spoken in the interviews to be able to read through those interviews as texts and identify pertinent coding themes present in the participants' stories, noting similarities and differences across the participants to help me solidify coding themes for analysis. In my second stage of coding, I transcribed each interview verbatim, I digitally highlighted certain words I noticed recurring in participant interviews. This is when my process of constant comparisons began. I quickly started to notice the ways in which some writers talked about their physical activity as a means to unlocking their creative potential, to think about their writing while away from their desk and moving. In my third stage of coding, once I had finished all data transcriptions, I printed every transcription and read through all transcripts together. Although I knew what participants had already stated, I wanted to spend several weeks in an open coding phase to reflect on the similarities and differences between their narratives, and as a result, I was able to see clear patterns of preference develop that would relegate participants to one of two states of writing—those that use exercise to generate ideas for writing and those that use exercise to restore their minds after writing sessions. Fourth, I took ten different-colored markers and I highlighted words, phrases, and sometimes whole paragraphs across transcripts where I located a potential theme that had been repeated or alluded to in other participants' interviews. The act of coding by way of highlighting helped me visualize the data better and in color, making glaringly obvious that some themes were occurring more frequently than others. At the end of this fourth coding stage, I realized that some of my participants clearly identified as being one of two particular kinds of writers using physical activities for one of two particular purposes, generative thinking or restorative thinking, both of which are terms I developed independent of existing scholarly frameworks to fit with the unique narrative descriptions shared by my participants. A few participants reported experiencing both generative and restorative thinking. For this fifth phase, I wrote each participant's name on a separate page in a yellow notebook. On each page, I wrote the name of the participant at the top of the page, listed each of the coding themes below her or his name, and then began to tally the number of times that theme occurred in the interview transcriptions. Using the ten themes I originally believed to be the most frequently recurring themes in this study, I then wrote an identifying word for the theme, highlighted the word with the color I used, and began to tally the number of instances in which a particular participant mentioned or alluded to that theme in her or his interview. What emerged demonstrates that the beliefs of these professional writers were often commonly shared ideas, further demonstrating similarities between the mindsets of these writers who run, walk, cycle, flow on a yoga mat, or play any sport on a regular basis. At the completion of this fifth stage, I reflected on how, although what is presented above offers shared themes, there seemed to be great variability in participants' experiences and descriptions of these themes.

Writing researchers Ann Blakeslee and Cathy Fleischer informed how I used feminist narrative(s) inquiry in conjunction with grounded methodology to code for themes. More specifically, in their book *Becoming a Writing Researcher,* Blakeslee and Fleischer advise that

> [s]ift through all of the material you've gathered, trying to find the themes that emerge from the multiple research strategies you used and then using those themes, along with other evidence you find, to answer your research questions. This is the moment to look both within each of the research strategies you used and across them (e.g., to analyze both what an individual interview tells you as well as what all of your interviews tell you). (166)

Looking within and across interviews helped me determine my coding themes. I then applied those coding themes in my analysis of professional and student writers. What became apparent was the prevalence of generative thinking, restorative thinking, and knowledge structuring.

CHALLENGES OF GROUNDED THEORY

Two challenges of working with this theory include the "data dilemma" and the "theory dilemma" (Farkas and Haas 84). Because this approach "provides little guidance in data collection," researchers have a tendency to go deep and wide in the[ir] collection of data" (Farkas and Haas 84). The "theory dilemma" occurs when there is a "mismatch between what a given theory would expect a researcher to find and what her data in fact reveal" (Farkas and Haas 84). Although I could have fallen prey to the data dilemma, I believe I did not. I chose interviews as my primary form of data, and the logs that could have been submitted in greater numbers would have been limited to four weeks' worth of logging per participant. I experienced the theory dilemma when I realized that the questions I created did not match well with the theories of flow I initially expected would explain the relationship between writing activity and physical activity. Eventually, I chose the terms for coding based on themes found in participant language because I wanted the "names of categories and codes [to be] drawn from the local terminology of site participants" (Farkas and Haas 83). Therefore, I devised the themes based on the collective language usage I witnessed my participants using, which was quite challenging because almost every participant could describe the relationship between physical activity and writing activity using several different terms or expressions. In so doing, I married the principles of feminist narrative(s) inquiry with the principles of grounded theory so that the voices of my participants were included and exerted influence on the analysis and results of this study.

Finally, as a teacher-researcher, I was guided by MacNealy's preference for seeking patterns and connections that might lead to interesting pedagogical recommendations, especially. One recommendation from MacNealy which I found especially useful is her strategy of self-examination. At the outset of my research on embodied writing in the classroom, I identified that I needed to conduct this research to better understand myself as a writer: my processes, habits, and preferences. MacNealy states: "One of the goals of a teacher who is also a researcher is to learn what about herself needs to change" (244). I have taken this recommendation to heart and employed it at every turn of this project. My intention as a teacher-researcher is to better understand my own embodied writing practices and how these embodied writing practices might be similar or different from the practices preferred by other writers. With such intentions in mind, I remained open to whatever themes or findings would arise from the data sets I collected, a stance supporting a grounded theory approach to methodological planning.

Appendix C

Interview Questions for Professional Writers

An interview with you may help the researchers uncover and collect varying descriptions of the relationship between writing activity and physical activity. Because the relationship may vary greatly from writer to writer, your answers could provide depth and breadth to the insights garnered in this study. Not all of the open-ended questions that follow will be asked of you, but the list that follows will give you a better sense of what to expect:

- Describe the typical physical activities you engage in during the workweek.
- Describe the typical physical activities you engage in on the weekends.
- Describe the physical activities you think you *perform* most successfully or efficiently.
- Describe the *practice* exercises you engage in to *perform* physical activity successfully or efficiently.
- How did you get *motivated* to begin practicing these physical activities?
- Describe any rituals you use or have used to motivate yourself during physical performances?
- Describe the physical activities that challenge your *imagination* the most.
- Describe when you feel most in *control* of your physical activity.
- Describe your current goals for your physical activity now or in the future.
- Describe the typical writing activities you engage in during the workweek.
- Describe the typical writing activities you engage in on the weekends.

- Describe the writing activities you think you *perform* most successfully or efficiently.

- Describe the *practice* exercises you engage in to *perform* writing activity successfully or efficiently.

- Describe any rituals you use or have used to motivate yourself during writing performances?

- How did you get *motivated* to begin practicing these writing activities?

- Describe the writing activities that challenge your *imagination* the most.

- Describe when you feel most in *control* of your writing activity.

- Describe your current goals for your writing activity now or in the future.

Interview Questions for Student Writers

An interview with you may help the research team uncover and collect varying descriptions of the relationship between writing activity and physical activity. Because the relationship may vary greatly from writer to writer, your answers could provide depth and breadth to the insights garnered in this study. Not all of the open-ended questions that follow will be asked of you, but the list that follows will give you a better sense of some questions you might be asked:

- Describe the typical physical activities you engage in during the workweek.

- Describe the typical physical activities you engage in on the weekends.

- Describe how logging impacted your physical activity.

- Describe when you feel most in control of or successful in your physical activity.

- Describe your current goals for your physical activity now or in the future.

- Describe the typical writing activities you engage in during the workweek.

- Describe the typical writing activities you engage in on the weekends.

- Describe how logging impacted your writing activity.

- Describe when you feel most in control of or successful in your writing activity.

- Describe your current goals for your writing activity now or in the future.

- Describe how you do or don't see physical activity and writing activity as related activities.

Index

About the Author

Dr. Jackie Hoermann-Elliott is an Assistant Professor of English and the Director of the First-Year Composition Program at Texas Woman's University. Her scholarship has been published in national journals, such as *Composition Forum*, and regional ones, such as Texas's *Conference of College Teachers of English Studies*. She attends several conferences regularly, including the Conference on College Composition and Communication, where she enjoys meeting other teachers who share her ardent interest in creativity and embodiment. Over a decade ago, her career as a writer began at *The Kansas City Star*, and since then she has written regularly for several other newspapers and magazines, including *The Des Moines Register, The Dallas Morning News, The Fort Worth Weekly*, and *Madeworthy Magazine*. In her free time, she can be found behind the handlebars of a bright yellow double Bob jogging stroller, pushing her two toddler sons through the rolling hills of Denton, Texas, or on a mat at an outdoor yoga class.

Photograph of the author by
Glen E. Ellman. Used by permission.

9 781643 172514